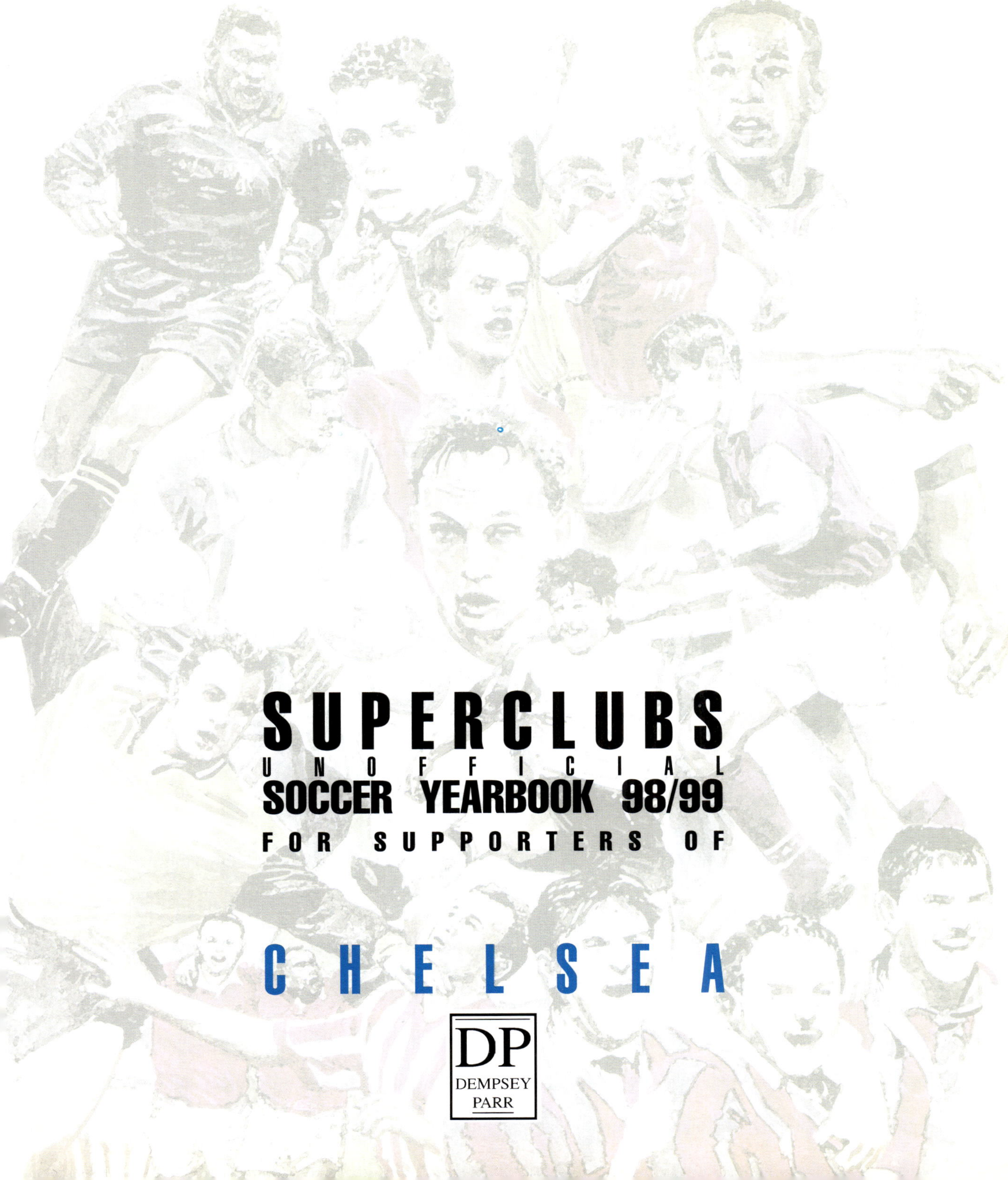

SUPERCLUBS

UNOFFICIAL

SOCCER YEARBOOK 98/99

FOR SUPPORTERS OF

CHELSEA

DP
DEMPSEY
PARR

First published in Great Britain in 1998 by
Dempsey Parr
13 Whiteladies Road
Clifton
Bristol BS8 1PB

ISBN: 1840840811

Produced for Dempsey Parr by
Prima Creative Services

Editorial director Roger Kean
Managing editor Tim Smith (Content E.D.B.)
Contributing authors
Steve Bradley
Jim Drewett (Deadline Features)
Steve Farragher
Sam Johnstone
Alex Leith (Deadline Features)
Rex Nash
Russell Smith
Tim Smith

Cover background and illustrations by Oliver Frey

Design and repro by Prima Creative Services

Printed and bound in Italy by L.E.G.O., Vicenza

Picture Acknowledgements
The publisher would like to thank the staff of Allsport and Action Images for their unstinting help and all the other libraries, newspapers and photographers who have made this edition possible. All pictures are credited alongside the photograph.

ALLSPORT: A MOMENT OF GLORY – THE 1997 FA CUP FINAL

SUPERCLUBS

UNOFFICIAL

SOCCER YEARBOOK 98/99

FOR SUPPORTERS OF

CHELSEA

CONTENTS

STATISTICS

For too many years the stylish under-achievers of London football, in the last two seasons Chelsea have put some serious silverware in the Stamford Bridge trophy cabinet. Currently the most cosmopolitan side in the Premiership, The Blues are also the only English club to have appointed successive foreign managers – Ruud Gullit and Gianluca Vialli. Between them the pair have helped to recreate the glory days of the early 1970s when Chelsea enjoyed a brief, but fondly-remembered, golden period.

BOTH: ALLSPORT

Date Formed: 1905
Date Entered Football League: 1905
Former Names: None
Official Nickname: The Blues (formerly The Pensioners)
Other Nicknames: None

MANAGERS SINCE JOINED LEAGUE:

Robertson	(1905–07)	Danny Blanchflower	(1978–79)
David Calderhead	(1907–33)	Geoff Hurst	(1979–81)
Leslie Knighton	(1933–39)	John Neal	(1981–85)
Billy Birrell	(1939–52)	John Hollins	(1985–88)
Ted Drake	(1952–61)	Bobby Campbell	(1988–91)
Tommy Docherty	(1962–67)	Ian Porterfield	(1991–93)
Dave Sexton	(1967–74)	David Webb	(1993)
Ron Suart	(1974–75)	Glenn Hoddle	(1993–96)
Eddie McCreadie	(1975–77)	Ruud Gullit	(1996–98)
Ken Shellito	(1977–78)	Gianluca Vialli	(1998–)

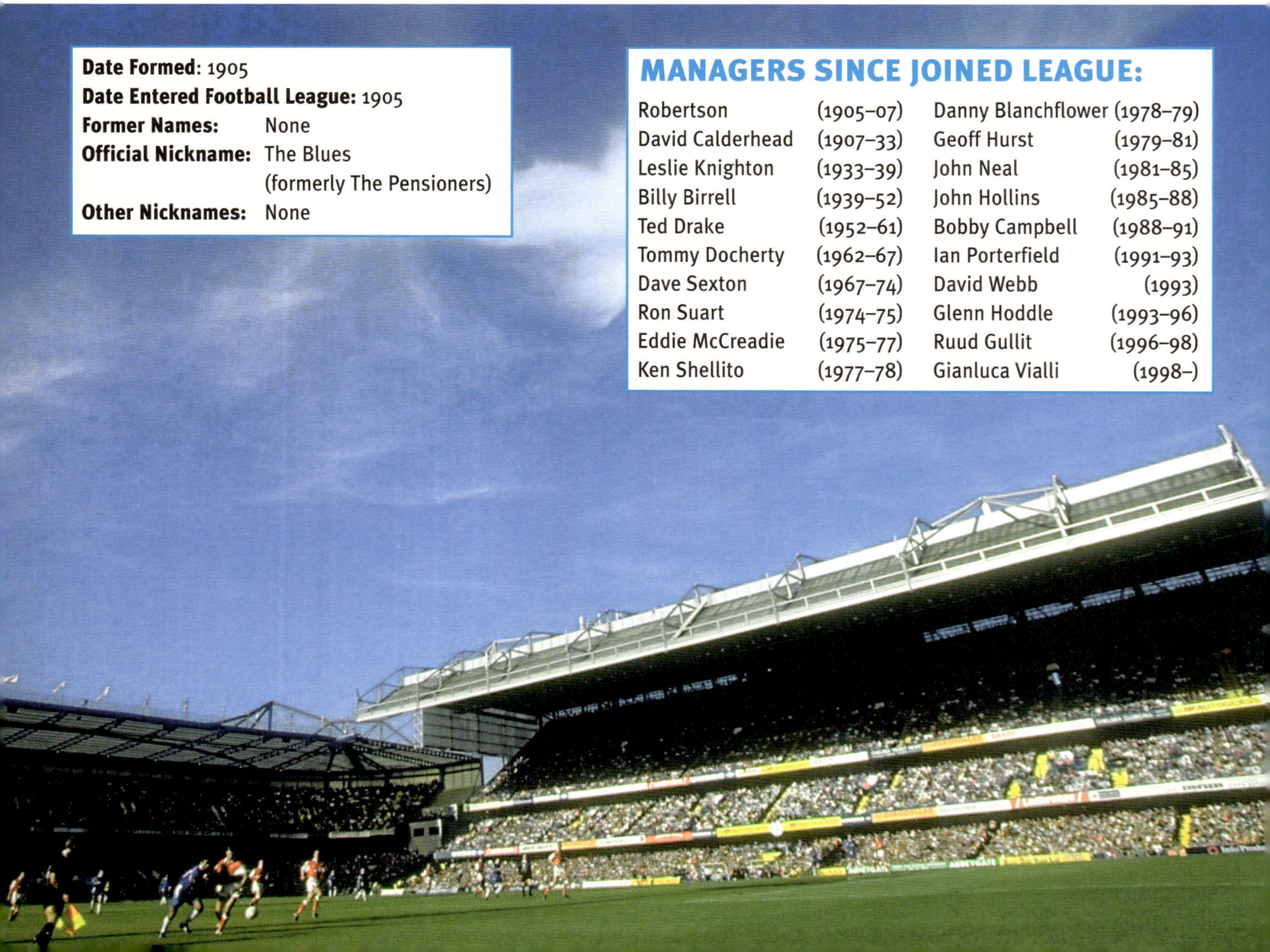

Player and manager, Vialli doesn't usually need a hand up to reach for his goals

CLUB HONOURS

Division One Champions
1955

Division Two Champions
1984, 1989

Division Two Runners-Up
1907, 1912, 1930, 1963, 1977

FA Cup Winners 1970 (April 29th, Old Trafford)
Chelsea v Leeds United 2–1 (aet); Scorers: Osgood, Webb
(After 2–2 draw April 11th, Wembley
Scorers: Houseman, Hutchinson)

FA Cup Winners 1997 (May 17th, Wembley)
Chelsea v Middlesbrough 2–0; Scorers: Di Matteo, Newton

FA Cup Runners-Up 1915 (April 24th, Old Trafford)
Chelsea v Sheffield United 0–3

FA Cup Runners-Up 1967 (May 20th, Wembley)
Chelsea v Tottenham Hotspur 1–2; Scorer: Tambling

FA Cup Runners-Up 1994 (May 14th, Wembley)
Chelsea v Manchester United 0–4

League Cup Winners 1965
(1st leg March 15th, Stamford Bridge)
Chelsea v Leicester City 3–2
Scorers: Tambling, Venables (pen), McCreadie
(2nd leg April 5th, Filbert Street)
Chelsea v Leicester City 0–0

League Cup Runners-Up 1972 (March 4th, Wembley)
Chelsea v Stoke City 2–1; Scorer: Osgood

League Cup Winners 1998 (March 29th, Wembley)
Chelsea v Middlesbrough 2–0 (aet)
Scorers: Sinclair, Di Matteo

Full Members' Cup Winners 1986 (March 23rd, Wembley)
Chelsea v Manchester City 5–4; Scorers: Lee (3), Speedie (2)

Zenith Data Systems Cup Winners 1990
(March 24th, Wembley)
Chelsea v Middlesbrough 1–0; Scorer: Dorigo

European Cup Winners' Cup Winners 1971
(May 21st, Piraeus, Greece)
Chelsea v Real Madrid 2–1; Scorers: Dempsey, Osgood
(After 1–1 draw, May 19th, Piraeus, Greece); Scorer: Osgood

European Cup Winners' Cup Winners 1998
(May 13th, Stockholm)
Chelsea v VFB Stuttgart 1–0; Scorer: Zola

ALLSPORT

| *Steve Clark fights it out with Manchester United's Andy Cole*

Stadiums: Stamford Bridge
Address: Stamford Bridge, Fulham Road, London SW6 1HS
Capacity: 34,850
Stands: Matthew Harding Stand, East Stand, West Stand, Shed Stand Family enclosure: Shed Stand (lower tier)
Prices: (1997-98) Adults (Category A): £21, £22, £25, £50; Children (Category A) : £9
Adults (Category B): £16, £17, £18, £50
Children (Category B): £7
Season ticket prices: Adult £345–£1,025
Children £185–£195
Parking facilities: None
Chairman: K.W. Bates
Club Sponsors: Autoglass

PITCH DIMENSIONS

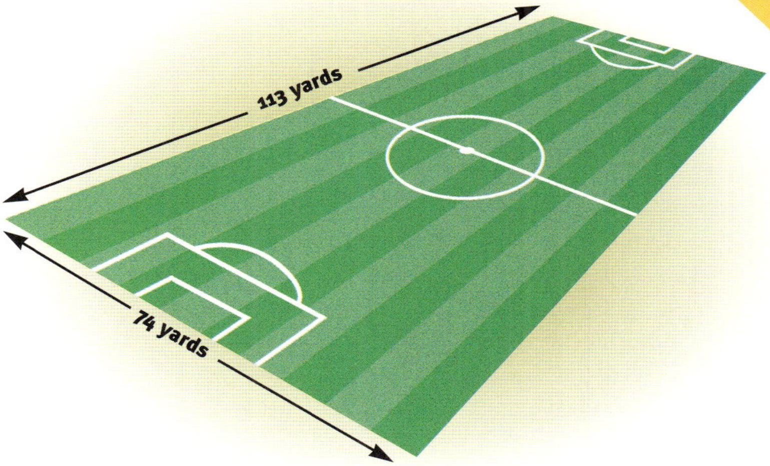

Record Attendance: 82,905 against Arsenal, Division 1, October 12th 1935

Preferred team formation: 4–4–2
Biggest rivals: Tottenham Hotspur

BEST PUB

Come The Revolution, 541 King's Head – a trendy bar a short distance from the ground with a pleasant garden at the back.

Programme: Chelsea Programme
Programme Editor: Neil Barnett
Programme Price: £2.50
Bus routes to stadium: 14,211
Tube Station: Fulham Broadway

FANZINES

The Chelsea Independent, PO Box 4027, London W9 3ZF
Red Card, 30 Harbourfield Rd, Banstead SM7 2DE
Cockney Rebel, 27 Dale St, London W4 2RJ

CONTACT NUMBERS

(Tel code 0171)

- Main number 385 5545
- Fax 381 4831
- Ticket Office 386 7799
- Matchday info 385 5545
- Commercial deparment 385 5545
- Supporters' Club 386 5557
- Club shop 565 1490
- Clubcall 0891 12 11 59

Michael Duberry gets one over on Everton's Duncan Ferguson

ALLSPORT

LEADING PLAYERS

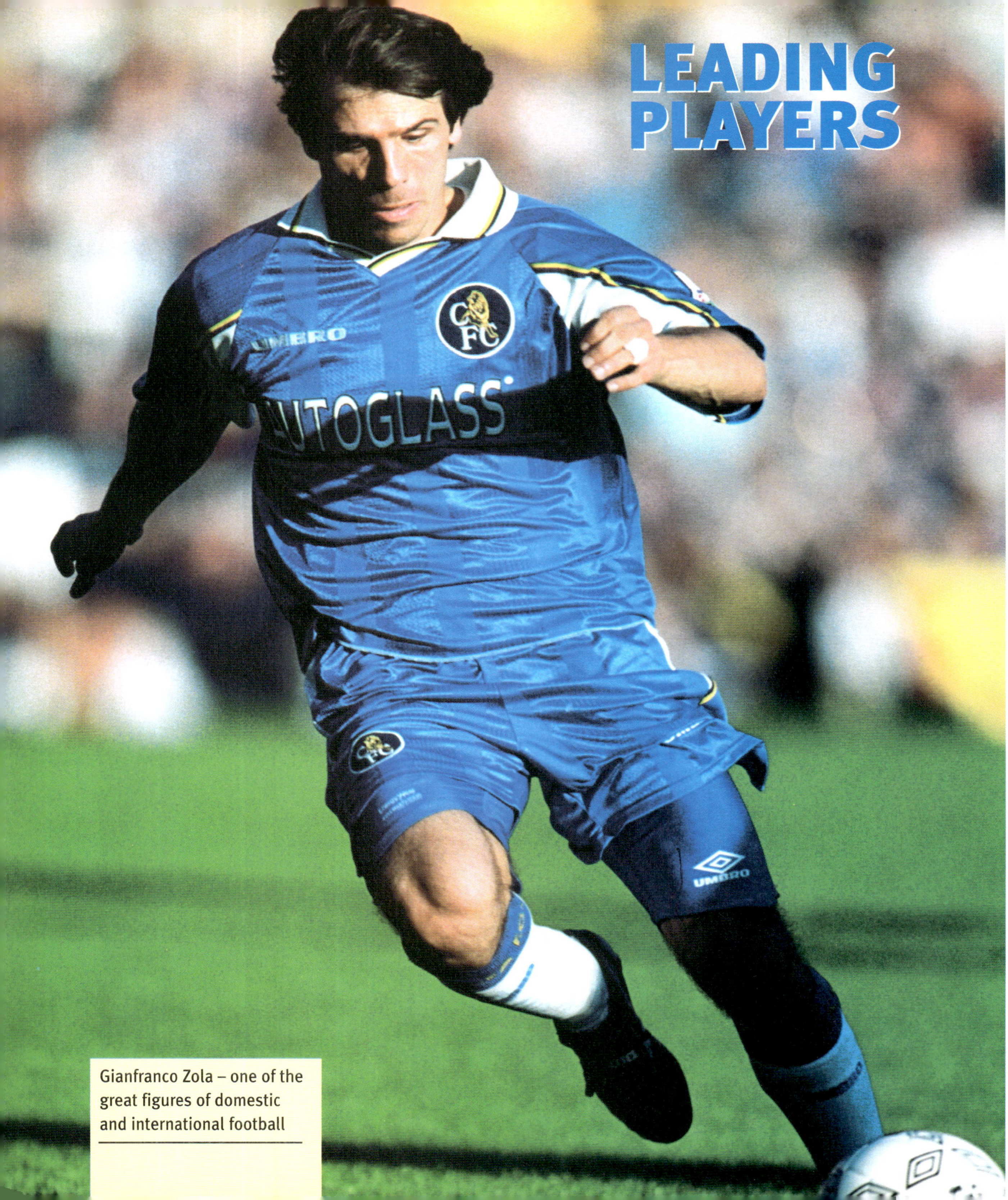

Gianfranco Zola – one of the great figures of domestic and international football

ALLSPORT

1997/98 SEASON TOP 10 GOALSCORERS

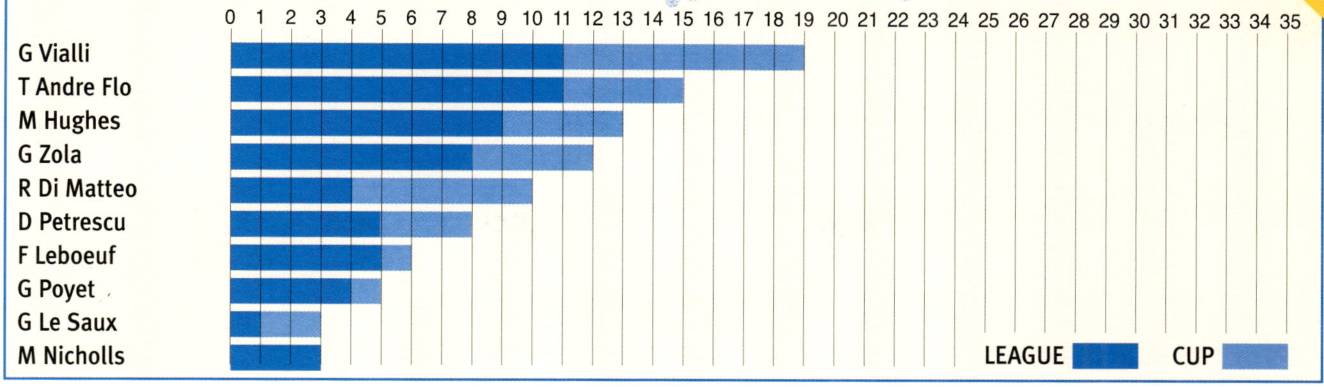

MOST LEAGUE APPEARANCES

PLAYER	APPEARANCES	SUBSTITUTE	GOALS
1 Tore Andre Flo	16	18	11
2 Frank Leboeuf	32	0	5
3 Dan Petrescu	31	0	5
4 Roberto Di Matteo	28	2	4
5 Mark Hughes	25	4	9
6 Ed De Goey	28	0	0
7 Gianfranco Zola	23	4	8
8 Steve Clarke	22	4	1
9 Graeme Le Saux	26	0	1
10 Dennis Wise	26	0	3
11 Michael Duberry	23	0	0
12 Frank Sinclair	20	2	1
13 Gianluca Vialli	14	7	11
14 Mark Nicholls	8	11	3
15 Eddie Newton	17	1	0
16 Gustavo Poyet	11	3	4
17 Danny Granville	9	4	0
18 Jody Morris	9	3	1
19 Andy Myers	11	1	0
20 Laurent Charvet	7	4	2

PLAYER STATISTICS

Record transfer fee paid:
Graeme Le Saux – £5,000,000 from Blackburn Rovers, August 1997

Record transfer fee received:
Gordon Durie – £2,200,000 from Tottenham Hotspur, July 1991

Oldest player: Dick Spence, 39 years, 1 month and 26 days against Bolton Wanderers, September 13th 1947

Youngest player: Ian 'Chico' Hamilton, 16 years, 4 months and 18 days against Tottenham Hotspur, March 18th 1967

International captains:
Peter Nicholas (Wales) 1989–91, Andy Townsend (Republic of Ireland) 1991–93, Paddy Mulligan, Andy Townsend (Republic of Ireland)

Most capped player:
Ray Wilkins, 24, England (1976–79)

SQUAD

ED DE GOEY

DOB: 20/12/66
Position: Goalkeeper
Squad number: 1
When joined club: June 1997 from Feyenoord
League Games played: 28
League Goals scored: 0
International caps: Holland (29)
League Debut: 9/8/97 v Coventry City (A)

DMITRI KHARINE

DOB: 16/8/68
Position: Goalkeeper
Squad number: 23
When joined club: December 1992 from CSKA Moscow
League Games played: 117
League Goals scored: 0
International caps: Russia, (34)
League Debut: 27/1/93 v QPR (A),

STEVE CLARKE

DOB: 29/8/63
Position: Defender
Squad number: 6
When joined club: January 1987 from St Mirren
League Games played: 330
League Goals scored: 7
International caps: Scotland, 6
League Debut: 24/1/87 v Norwich City (A)

MICHAEL DUBERRY

DOB: 14/10/75
Position: Defender
Squad number: 12
When joined club: July 1993 from trainee
League Games played: 61
League Goals scored: 1
International caps: 0
League Debut: 4/5/94 v Coventry City (H)

ALLSPORT

Leicester's Tony Cotte tries huffing and puffing Michael Duberry off the ball

With the grace of a gazelle, Zola aims for the ball, otherwise it's a double-hammer for Spurs' John Scales

ALLSPORT

DANNY GRANVILLE

DOB: 19/1/75
Position: Defender
Squad number: 17
When joined club: March 1997 from Cambridge United
League Games played: 18
League Goals scored: 0
International caps: 0
League Debut: 5/4/96 v Arsenal (H)

FRANK LEBOEUF

DOB: 22/1/68
Position: Defender
Squad number: 5
When joined club: June 1996 from Strasbourg
League Games played: 58
League Goals scored: 11
International caps: France, (11)
League Debut: 18/8/96 v Southampton (A)

GRAEME LE SAUX

DOB: 17/10/68
Position: Defender
Squad number: 14
When joined club: December 1987 from St Paul's, Jersey and August 1997 from Blackburn Rovers
League Games played: 116
League Goals scored: 9
International caps: England, 20
League Debut: 13/5/89 v Portsmouth (A)

ANDY MYERS

DOB: 3/11/73
Position: Defender
Squad number: 18
When joined club: June 1991 from trainee
League Games played: 82
League Goals scored: 2
International caps: 0
League Debut: 6/4/91 v Luton Town (H)

The £5 million Chelsea laid out to Blackburn Rovers for Graeme Le Saux at the beginning of the last season, appears to have paid off

ALLSPORT

JODY MORRIS
DOB: 22/12/78
Position: Midfielder
Squad number: 28
When joined club: Decemeber 1995 from trainee
League Games played: 25
League Goals scored: 1
International caps: 0
League Debut: 4/2/96 v Middlesbrough

EDDIE NEWTON
DOB: 13/12/71
Position: Midfielder
Squad number: 24
When joined club: May 1990 from trainee
League Games played: 158
League Goals scored: 8
International caps: 0
League Debut: 2/5/92 v Everton (A)

DAN PETRESCU
DOB: 22/12/67
Position: Midfielder
Squad number: 2
When joined club: November 1995 from Sheffield Wednesday
League Games played: 89
League Goals scored: 10
International caps: Romania (64)
League Debut: 18/11/95 v Leeds United (A)

FRANK SINCLAIR
DOB: 3/12/71
Position: Defender
Squad number: 20
League Games played: 169
League Goals scored: 7
International caps: 5, Jamaica
League Debut: 6/4/91 v Luton Town (H)

ROBERTO DI MATTEO
DOB: 29/5/70
Position: Midfielder
Squad number: 16
When joined club: July 1996 from Lazio
League Games played: 64
League Goals scored: 11
International caps: Italy (20)
League Debut: 18/8/96 v Southampton (A)

GUSTAVO POYET
DOB: 15/11/67
Position: Midfielder
Squad number: 8
When joined club: July 1997 from Zaragoza
League Games played: 14
League Goals scored: 4
International caps: Uruguay (30)
League Debut: 9/8/97 v Coventry City (A)

Player or manager? Gianluca Vialli did a little less of the former at the end of last season but a whole load of the latter in a year that saw Chelsea take the European Cup Winners' Cup

ALLSPORT

MARK HUGHES

DOB: 1/11/63
Position: Striker
Squad number: 10
When joined club: July 1995 from Manchester United
League Games played: 98
League Goals scored: 25
International caps: Wales (65)
League Debut: 19/8/95 v Everton (H)

MARK NICHOLLS

DOB: 30/5/77
Position: Striker
Squad number: 22
When joined club: July 1995 from trainee
League Games played: 27
League Goals scored: 3
International caps: 0
League Debut: 12/10/96 v Leicester City (A)

DENNIS WISE

DOB: 16/12/66
Position: Midfielder
Squad number: 11
When joined club: July 1990 from Wimbledon
League Games played: 244
League Goals scored: 46
International caps: England (12)
League Debut: 25/8/90 v Derby County (H)

GIANLUCA VIALLI

DOB: 9/7/64
Position: Striker
Squad number: 9
When joined club: May 1966 from Juventus
League Games played: 42
League Goals scored: 20
International caps: Italy (59)
League Debut: 18/8/96 v Southampton (A)

TORE ANDRE FLO

DOB: 15/6/73
Position: Striker
Squad number: 19
When joined club: July 1997 from Brann Bergen
League Games played: 34
League Goals scored: 11
International caps: Norway (20)
League Debut: 9/8/97 v Coventry City (A)

GIANFRANCO ZOLA

DOB: 5/7/66
Position: Striker
Squad number: 25
When joined club: November 1996 from Parma
League Games played: 50
League Goals scored: 16
International caps: Italy (33)
League Debut: 16/11/96 v Blackburn rovers (A)

ALL-TIME RECORDS

1997/98 SEASON FINAL POSITIONS

POINTS 10 20 30 40 50 60 70 80 90 100 200 300 400 500

Club	Points	Goals	Average position in the Premier League since joining	Average position by points in the league since joining	Average position by goals in the league since joining
Arsenal	4543	6168	5	3	12
Aston Villa	4463	6549	6	4	1
Blackburn Rovers	4372	6183	4	8	11
Charlton Athletic	3259	4453	20	65	60
Chelsea	3758	5087	8	36	34
Coventry City	3196	4273	17	67	67
Derby County	4329	6249	10	10	8
Everton	4455	6306	16	5	6
Leeds United	3522	4475	7	43	58
Leicester City	4027	5796	14	24	19
Liverpool	4801	6457	2	1	3
Manchester United	4710	6402	1	2	5
Middlesbrough	3990	5615	19	26	26
Newcastle United	4308	6436	3	14	4
Nottingham Forest	4230	5707	15	19	22
Sheffield Wednesday	4231	5887	12	18	17
Southampton	3274	4545	18	61	53
Tottenham Hotspur	3794	5383	9	35	28
West Ham United	3369	3355	13	57	80
Wimbledon	1220	1259	11	88	88

3 Average position in the Premier League since joining

92 Average position by points in the league since joining (includes 2 points for a win and 3 points for a win)

92 Average position by goals in the league since joining

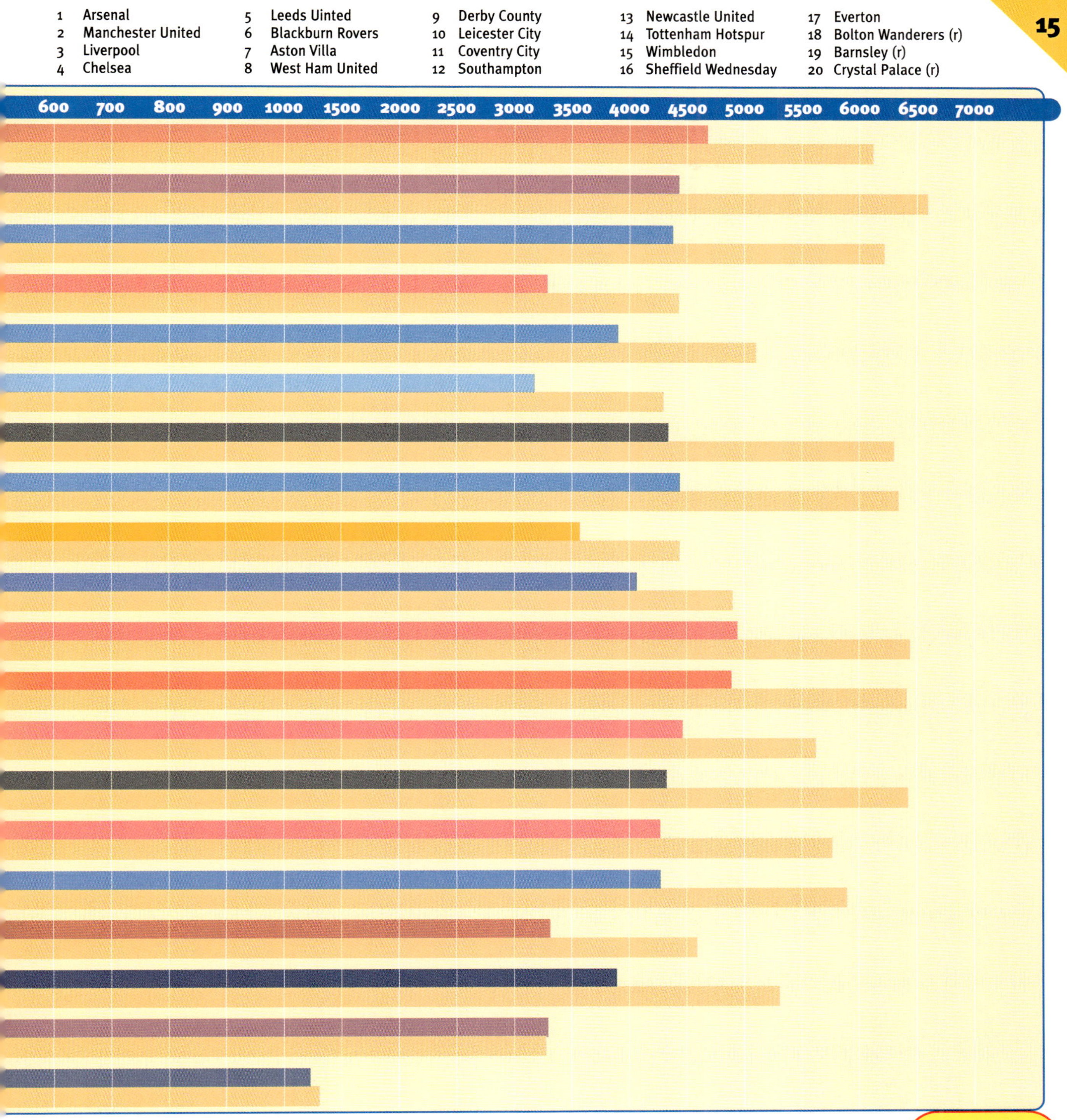

Chelsea's total points since joining league.. 3758

Stamford Bridge: home of Chelsea
AEROFILMS

SUPERCLUBS

UNOFFICIAL

SOCCER YEARBOOK 98/99

JULY 1998 – JUNE 1999 DIARY AND CLUB FIXTURES

Fixture dates are subject to change. FA Cup draws were not made at press-time.

THE STORY OF PREMIER LEAGUE SOCCER IN THE 1997/98 SEASON

FOR SUPPORTERS OF

CHELSEA

ENGLISH PREMIERSHIP CLUB ADDRESSES

ARSENAL
Arsenal Stadium, Highbury, London, N5 1BU
Main No: 0171 704 4000

ASTON VILLA
Villa Park, Trinity Road Stand, North Stand, Doug Ellis Road
Main No: 0121 327 2299

BLACKBURN ROVERS
Ewood Park, Blackburn, BB2 4JF
Main No: 01254 698888

CHARLTON ATHLETIC
The Valley, Floyd Road, Charlton, London, SE7 8BL
Main No: 0181 333 4000

CHELSEA
Stamford Bridge, Fulham Road, London, SW6 1HS
Main No: 0171 385 5545

COVENTRY CITY
Highfield Road Stadium, King Richard Street, Coventry, CV2 4FW
Main No: 01203 234000

DERBY COUNTY
Pride Park Stadium, Derby, DE24 8XL
Main No: 01332 667503

EVERTON
Goodison Park, Liverpool, L4 4EL
Main No: 0151 330 2200

LEEDS UNITED
Elland Road, Leeds, West Yorkshire, LS11 OES
Main No: 0113 226 6000

LEICESTER
Filbert Street, Leicester, LE2 7FL
Main No: 0116 291 5000

LIVERPOOL
Anfield Road, Liverpool. L4 OTH
Main No: 0151 263 2361

MANCHESTER UNITED
Old Trafford, Manchester
Main No: 0161 872 1661 & 0161 930 1968

MIDDLESBROUGH
Cellnet Riverside Stadium, Middlesbrough, Cleveland, TS3 6RS
Main No: 01642 877 700

NEWCASTLE UNITED
St James' Park, Newcastle-Upon-Tyne, NE1 4ST
Main No: 0191 201 8400

NOTTINGHAM FOREST
City Ground, Nottingham, NG2 5FJ
Main No: 0115 982 4444

SHEFFIELD WEDNESDAY
Hillsborough, Sheffield, S6 1SW
Main No: 0114 221 2121

SOUTHAMPTON
The Dell, Milton Road, Southampton, SO9 4XX
Main No: 01703 220505

TOTTENHAM HOTSPUR
White Hart Lane, 748 High Road, Tottenham, London, N17 OAP
Main No: 0181 365 5000

WEST HAM UNITED
Boleyn Ground, Green Street, Upton Park, London, E13 9AZ
Main No: 0181 542 2748

WIMBLEDON
Selhurst Park Stadium, Wimbledon
Main No: 0181 771 2233

ALL-CLUB LOCATIONS

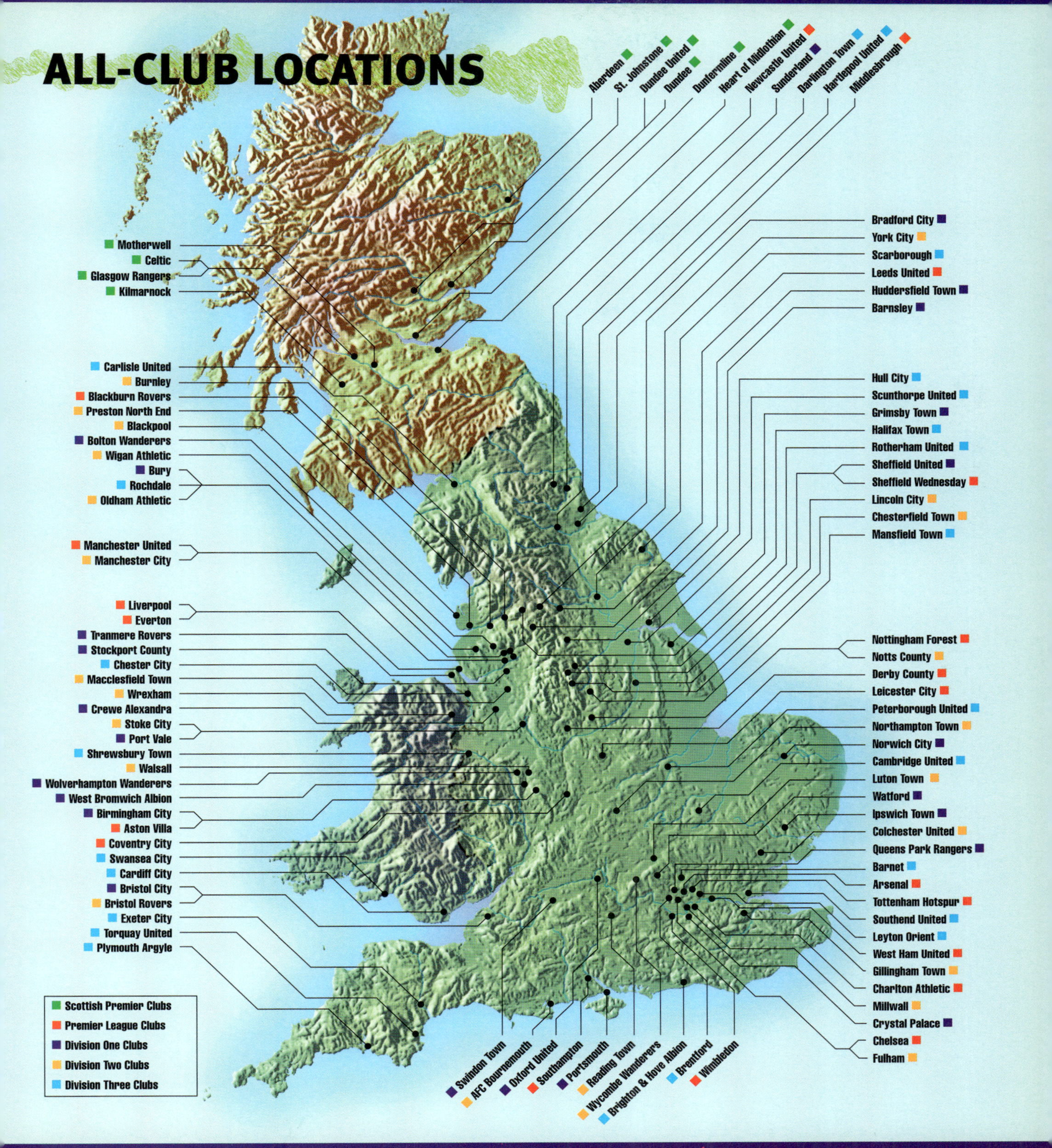

CALENDAR 1998

January

	M	T	W	T	F	S	S
1				1	2	3	4
2	5	6	7	8	9	10	11
3	12	13	14	15	16	17	18
4	19	20	21	22	23	24	25
5	26	27	28	29	30	31	

February

	M	T	W	T	F	S	S
5							1
6	2	3	4	5	6	7	8
7	9	10	11	12	13	14	15
8	16	17	18	19	20	21	22
9	23	24	25	26	27	28	

March

	M	T	W	T	F	S	S
9							1
10	2	3	4	5	6	7	8
11	9	10	11	12	13	14	15
12	16	17	18	19	20	21	22
13	23	24	25	26	27	28	29
14	30	31					

April

	M	T	W	T	F	S	S
14			1	2	3	4	5
15	6	7	8	9	10	11	12
16	13	14	15	16	17	18	19
17	20	21	22	23	24	25	26
18	27	28	29	30			

May

	M	T	W	T	F	S	S
18					1	2	3
19	4	5	6	7	8	9	10
20	11	12	13	14	15	16	17
21	18	19	20	21	22	23	24
22	25	26	27	28	29	30	31

June

	M	T	W	T	F	S	S
23	1	2	3	4	5	6	7
24	8	9	10	11	12	13	14
25	15	16	17	18	19	20	21
26	22	23	24	25	26	27	28
27	29	30					

July

	M	T	W	T	F	S	S
27			1	2	3	4	5
28	6	7	8	9	10	11	12
29	13	14	15	16	17	18	19
30	20	21	22	23	24	25	26
31	27	28	29	30	31		

August

	M	T	W	T	F	S	S
31						1	2
32	3	4	5	6	7	8	9
33	10	11	12	13	14	15	16
34	17	18	19	20	21	22	23
35	24	25	26	27	28	29	30
36	31						

September

	M	T	W	T	F	S	S
36		1	2	3	4	5	6
37	7	8	9	10	11	12	13
38	14	15	16	17	18	19	20
39	21	22	23	24	25	26	27
40	28	29	30				

October

	M	T	W	T	F	S	S
40				1	2	3	4
41	5	6	7	8	9	10	11
42	12	13	14	15	16	17	18
43	19	20	21	22	23	24	25
44	26	27	28	29	30	31	

November

	M	T	W	T	F	S	S
44							1
45	2	3	4	5	6	7	8
46	9	10	11	12	13	14	15
47	16	17	18	19	20	21	22
48	23	24	25	26	27	28	29
49	30						

December

	M	T	W	T	F	S	S
49		1	2	3	4	5	6
50	7	8	9	10	11	12	13
51	14	15	16	17	18	19	20
52	21	22	23	24	25	26	27
53	28	29	30	31			

UK Holiday   Scotland Holiday   N. Ireland Holiday   Not in Scotland

CALENDAR 1999

January

	M	T	W	T	F	S	S
1					1	2	3
2	4	5	6	7	8	9	10
3	11	12	13	14	15	16	17
4	18	19	20	21	22	23	24
5	25	26	27	28	29	30	31

February

	M	T	W	T	F	S	S
6	1	2	3	4	5	6	7
7	8	9	10	11	12	13	14
8	15	16	17	18	19	20	21
9	22	23	24	25	26	27	28

March

	M	T	W	T	F	S	S
10	1	2	3	4	5	6	7
11	8	9	10	11	12	13	14
12	15	16	17	18	19	20	21
13	22	23	24	25	26	27	28
14	29	30	31				

April

	M	T	W	T	F	S	S
14				1	2	3	4
15	5	6	7	8	9	10	11
16	12	13	14	15	16	17	18
17	19	20	21	22	23	24	25
18	26	27	28	29	30		

May

	M	T	W	T	F	S	S
18						1	2
19	3	4	5	6	7	8	9
20	10	11	12	13	14	15	16
21	17	18	19	20	21	22	23
22	24	25	26	27	28	29	30
23	31						

June

	M	T	W	T	F	S	S
23		1	2	3	4	5	6
24	7	8	9	10	11	12	13
25	14	15	16	17	18	19	20
26	21	22	23	24	25	26	27
27	28	29	30				

July

	M	T	W	T	F	S	S
27				1	2	3	4
28	5	6	7	8	9	10	11
29	12	13	14	15	16	17	18
30	19	20	21	22	23	24	25
31	26	27	28	29	30	31	

August

	M	T	W	T	F	S	S
31							1
32	2	3	4	5	6	7	8
33	9	10	11	12	13	14	15
34	16	17	18	19	20	21	22
35	23	24	25	26	27	28	29
36	30	31					

September

	M	T	W	T	F	S	S
36			1	2	3	4	5
37	6	7	8	9	10	11	12
38	13	14	15	16	17	18	19
39	20	21	22	23	24	25	26
40	27	28	29	30			

October

	M	T	W	T	F	S	S
40					1	2	3
41	4	5	6	7	8	9	10
42	11	12	13	14	15	16	17
43	18	19	20	21	22	23	24
44	25	26	27	28	29	30	31

November

	M	T	W	T	F	S	S
45	1	2	3	4	5	6	7
46	8	9	10	11	12	13	14
47	15	16	17	18	19	20	21
48	22	23	24	25	26	27	28
49	29	30					

December

	M	T	W	T	F	S	S
49			1	2	3	4	5
50	6	7	8	9	10	11	12
51	13	14	15	16	17	18	19
52	20	21	22	23	24	25	26
53	27	28	29	30	31		

Monday June 29 1998

Tuesday June 30 1998

Wednesday July 1 1998

Thursday July 2 1998

Friday July 3 1998

Saturday July 4 1998

Sunday July 5 1998

Monday July 6 1998

Tuesday July 7 1998

Wednesday July 8 1998

Thursday July 9 1998

Friday July 10 1998

Saturday July 11 1998

Sunday July 12 1998

V

9 August, 199. 7After a wait of 110 years, Barnsley finally arrived in England's top division. And the press trotted out the predictable clichés. All the talk was of 'plucky Barnsley', dour but cheerful working class folk and brass bands. 'West Ham and Chelsea at home, Palace away – that's a nine-point start to the season,' offered optimistic professional Yorkshireman Michael Parkinson. Neil Redfearn nodded home Barnsley's Premiership opener in the ninth minute, but West Ham spoiled the party with two second-half strikes from Hartson and Lampard.

ALLSPORT

Barnsley fans enjoying the opening day of the Premiership

Teddy Sheringham's return to White Hart Lane on 10 August was an eventful occasion. The former Tottenham hero, now in the red of Manchester United after his £3.5 million summer switch, was booed and jeered mercilessly throughout by Spurs fans. Teddy had the opportunity to ram the taunts down their throats after Justin Edinburgh handled in the area in the 60th minute, but his spot-kick struck the post, much to the delight of the majority of the gathered 26,359. But Teddy's blushes were saved after United registered twice in two minutes. Nicky Butt scored from 12 yards in the 82nd minute, and 60 seconds later David Beckham's cross deflected off Ramon Vega and rolled past Ian Walker.

Teddy Sheringham missing the penalty at White Hart Lane

ALLSPORT

1998 July 13 – July 26

Monday July 13 1998

Tuesday July 14 1998

Wednesday July 15 1998

Thursday July 16 1998

Friday July 17 1998

Saturday July 18 1998

Sunday July 19 1998

Monday July 20 1998

Tuesday July 21 1998

Wednesday July 22 1998

Thursday July 23 1998

Friday July 24 1998

Saturday July 25 1998

Sunday July 26 1998

West Ham may have spoilt Barnsley's Premiership party on the opening day, but the South Yorkshire side took their revenge on the capital when they played against Crystal Palace at Selhurst Park on 12 August. Neil Redfearn, Barnsley's scorer against West Ham, struck a ferocious, dipping left-foot shot from 30 yards early in the second half and it proved enough for the Yorkshiremen to take the points north. New Palace hero Attilio Lombardo made little impression, despite his two-goal salvo at Goodison Park on the opening day. And manager Steve Coppell fined the Italian for turning up late. 'I didn't realise the traffic would be so thick in London,' offered Palace's own Bald Eagle.

ALLSPORT

Tykes starman, Neil Redfearn

The following day Aston Villa were put to the sword by a stunning first-half hat-trick from Blackburn's rejuvenated striker Chris Sutton. Roy Hodgson had instilled a real sense of belief in his short time as manager after the summer switch from Inter Milan, and Blackburn were rampant against an out-of-sorts Villa. Sutton registered three times in the opening 45 minutes and completely outshone his opposite number, seven-million-pound man Stan Collymore. With wingers Wilcox and Ripley raiding the flanks, Blackburn constantly offered a threat to the Villa defence. Sutton's first was the best of the three, the former Norwich man volleying home a Stuart Ripley centre from just inside the area.

Chris Sutton completing his first-half hat-trick

ALLSPORT

Monday July 27 1998

Tuesday July 28 1998

Wednesday July 29 1998

Thursday July 30 1998

Friday July 31 1998

Saturday August 1 1998

Sunday August 2 1998

Monday August 3 1998

Tuesday August 4 1998

Wednesday August 5 1998

Thursday August 6 1998

Friday August 7 1998

Saturday August 8 1998

Sunday August 9 1998

Tottenham secured their first victory of the season against Derby County on 23 August, much to the relief of their beleaguered boss Gerry Francis. With the gentlemen of the press predicting Francis as favourite to be the season's first Premiership managerial casualty, the Spurs boss was looking increasingly desperate, particularly with the signings of wingers David Ginola and José Dominguez. But Dominguez, a first-half substitute for injured Frenchman Ginola, shone on his debut, lifting the White Hart Lane faithful with his wizardry. Stefan Eranio's foul on the Portuguese winger led to the Spurs goal, Colin Calderwood heading home Sinton's resultant free-kick.

ALLSPORT

José Dominguez added zip to Spurs' early season

Barnsley's second home Premiership fixture on 24 August left them in no doubt about the task they faced in retaining their position in the top division. Chelsea's team of all-stars led the Yorkshiremen a merry dance with Gianluca Vialli helping himself to four goals in their 6–0 victory. Vialli, recalled in place of Mark Hughes, struck just before half-time and found the net three times after the interval in his finest performance since his transfer from Juventus. 'They toyed with us,' said Barnsley manager Danny Wilson, putting on as brave a face as he could muster.

Vialli had plenty to celebrate at the end of August 1997. Little did he know that within another seven months, he would have even more...

ALLSPORT

Monday August 10 1998

Tuesday August 11 1998

Wednesday August 12 1998

Thursday August 13 1998

Friday August 14 1998

Saturday August 15 1998
Chelsea at Coventry City

Sunday August 16 1998

Monday August 17 1998

Tuesday August 18 1998

Wednesday August 19 1998

Thursday August 20 1998

Friday August 21 1998

Saturday August 22 1998
Newcastle United at Chelsea

Sunday August 23 1998

25 August: Blackburn's fixture against Sheffield Wednesday was hardly a mouth-watering prospect but it turned into one of the most astonishing Premiership games of the season. A fiery Blackburn ripped into the Wednesday defence from the off and after 24 minutes the score was 5–1 to Roy Hodgson's side. Scottish striker Kevin Gallacher scored twice in the first seven minutes before Wednesday's Carbone pulled one back. But the Lancashiremen had it wrapped up by half-time with strikes from Sutton, Wilcox and an own-goal from Graham Hyde. The second half wasn't without incident, either. Blackburn keeper John Filan was carried off with a broken arm, and Benito Carbone scored a brilliant 30-yarder before being sent off for headbutting.

ALLSPORT

Calm down Wrighty... again

27 August: Dennis Bergkamp continued his magnificent start to the season with a stunning hat-trick, but once again it was his strike partner Ian Wright who made all the headlines. Arsenal were winning 2–1 in the 90th minute but incredibly the score finished 3–3, with Leicester's Steve Walsh heading home deep into time added on. After the final whistle, there was an unseemly melee, which resulted in Wright, Patrick Vieira, Steve Walsh and Arsenal coach Pat Rice being reported to the FA. All were later cleared.

Kevin Gallacher masterfully handled by Des Walker

ALLSPORT

ALLSPORT

Above: David Hopkin brings Bremner-like attitude to Leeds and Scotland

Perennial World Cup qualifiers Scotland continued their impressive progress towards France 98 with a 4–1 victory over Belarus on 7 September. Leeds' David Hopkin, a second-half substitute for Scottish captain Gary McAllister of Coventry, opened his international account with two impressive strikes. In-form Blackburn Rovers striker Kevin Gallacher also scored a brace. The victory took Scotland back to the top of Group Four above Austria and ensured they would be guaranteed at least second spot and a play-off place.

1 September: Newly promoted Bolton Wanderers were one of two Premiership teams starting the season in a new stadium. But unlike Derby County, the Lancastrians had thus far been unable to christen the opulent £35 million Reebok Stadium with a goal. Surely with Everton the visitors their luck would change? In the 53rd minute, Bolton's Gerry Taggart nodded the ball just over the line, as TV replays later confirmed, but referee Stephen Lodge over-ruled. And the evening got worse for Bolton when their record signing, Robbie Elliot, was stretchered off with a broken leg. The game finished 0–0.

Right: Reebok Stadium

Quiz 1 About Chelsea

1. **What is the connection between Chelsea and Piccadilly Undergound station?**
   a) It was the tube station that Chelsea returned to after the 1970 FA Cup Final
   b) Dirt from the creation of the station was used in the original Stamford Bridge embankments
   c) Ken Bates owns part of the underground station

2. **Chelsea's first home game was against Hull in 1905. What was the score?**
   a) 5–1 to Chelsea
   b) 5–1 to Hull
   c) 0–0

Allsport

3. **Where was legendary 22-stone keeper William 'Fatty' Foulkes signed from?**
   a) Sheffield United
   b) Sheffield Wednesday
   c) Spurs

4. **Who scored in Chelsea's 1971 European Cup Winners' Cup victory over Real Madrid?**
   a) Cooke and Hutchinson
   b) Cooke and Dempsey
   c) Osgood and Dempsey

5. **What stopped Chelsea playing in their first European Cup in 1955?**
   a) Injuries to key players
   b) Inability to raise the cash to travel
   c) The English FA refused them permission to play

6. **Chelsea were promoted from Division Two to Division One for the first time in 1907. What was the score in their first game of the season?**
   a) 9–2 win against Glossop
   b) 2–9 loss against Manchester United
   c) 2–2 draw with Arsenal

7. **What was significant about the Chelsea v Spurs 1967 FA Cup Final?**
   a) Spurs were awarded their place when their semi-final opponents dropped out
   b) It was the first all-London final this century
   c) Chelsea played in red

8. **Who scored the first equaliser in the 1970 FA Cup Final?**
   a) Peter Houseman
   b) Peter Osgood
   c) Charlie Cooke

9. **Why did Dave Sexton transfer list Peter Osgood in 1972?**
   a) 'Lack of effort'
   b) 'Too old'
   c) Osgood requested it

10. **Who took over from Peter Bonnetti in goal against Coventry on 18 December, 1972?**
    a) Ron Harris
    b) Peter Osgood
    c) David Webb

Answers: 1.b 2.a 3.a 4.c 5.c 6.a 7.b 8.a 9.a 10.c

Monday August 24 1998

Tuesday August 25 1998

Wednesday August 26 1998

Thursday August 27 1998

Friday August 28 1998

Saturday August 29 1998

Sunday August 30 1998

Monday August 31 1998

Tuesday September 1 1998

Wednesday September 2 1998

Thursday September 3 1998

Friday September 4 1998

Saturday September 5 1998

Sunday September 6 1998

Paul Gascoigne produced his most impressive international performance since Euro 96 in England's emphatic 4–0 victory over Moldova in the World Cup qualifier on 10 September. Despite the poor quality of the opposition, Gascoigne dominated with a superb display of passing and dribbling, capped by a late goal. Paul Scholes opened England's account with a spectacular diving header from a David Beckham cross and Ian Wright weighed in with the other two. England went into the game knowing that if they beat Moldova, they would only need to draw against Italy in Rome, after the Italians failed to beat Georgia.

ALLSPORT

Paul Gascoigne scoring against Moldova

Leeds ended a run of three straight defeats with a victory over Blackburn Rovers in another astonishing game at Ewood Park on 14 September. Three weeks earlier, Rovers had slaughtered Sheffield Wednesday 7–2, but this time the team from the west side of the Pennines refused to roll over. All seven goals came in a frantic first 33 minutes as Leeds raced to a 4–3 lead that they held on to until the end. The best strikes came from Rod Wallace and Kevin Gallacher, the latter a flashing 25-yard drive. 'It was great for the fans but the standard of defending was awful from both teams,' said a relieved George Graham afterwards.

Rod Wallace, Leeds favourite, shows his class against Blackburn

ALLSPORT

Monday September 7 1998

Tuesday September 8 1998

Wednesday September 9 1998
Arsenal at Chelsea

Thursday September 10 1998

Friday September 11 1998

Saturday September 12 1998
Nottingham Forest at Chelsea

Sunday September 13 1998

Monday September 14 1998

Tuesday September 15 1998

Wednesday September 16 1998

Thursday September 17 1998

Friday September 18 1998

Saturday September 19 1998

Sunday September 20 1998

A big week for British teams in Europe began with one of the most eagerly awaited games for years, when Celtic met Liverpool at Parkhead in the first round of the UEFA Cup on 16 September. Liverpool whizzkid Michael Owen stunned the 48,526 crowd when he finished with coolness beyond his years in the sixth minute. But Celtic replied with two second-half strikes and seemed certain to take a 2–1 lead to Anfield for the second leg. That was until Steve McManaman picked up the ball well inside his own half and proceeded to dribble the length of the field before slotting past Jonathan Gould (a recent signing from Bradford and Celtic's third-choice keeper) into the Celtic net.

ALLSPORT

'Macca' disrupts the Celtic-Liverpool camaraderie

Newcastle United finally realised their dream of playing in the Champions' League when they welcomed visitors Barcelona to St James' Park on 17 September. Roared on by a capacity crowd, the Geordies tore into the Spanish giants with Tino Asprilla scoring two first-half goals to give them a 2–0 lead at the interval. Asprilla completed his hat-trick after the break, but when Barcelona scored two late goals, it was Newcastle who found themselves praying for the whistle. 'The best game in recent times in Europe,' reckoned Kenny Dalglish.

Tino's biggest game of the season. Against Barca he was awesome

ALLSPORT

Monday September 21 1998
Chelsea at Blackburn Rovers

Tuesday September 22 1998

Wednesday September 23 1998

Thursday September 24 1998

Friday September 25 1998

Saturday September 26 1998
Middlesbrough at Chelsea

Sunday September 27 1998

Monday September 28 1998

Tuesday September 29 1998

Wednesday September 30 1998

Thursday October 1 1998

Friday October 2 1998

Saturday October 3 1998

Sunday October 4 1998
Chelsea at Liverpool

> Republic of Ireland skipper Roy Keane suffered a devastating knee injury in Manchester United's first defeat of the campaign at Leeds on 27 September. Keane fell to the ground after a clumsy challenge on Leeds' Norwegian international Alf-Inge Haaland. Keane was shown the yellow card by referee Martin Bodenham and promptly limped off only to find the injury would keep him out for the rest of the season. The hard-fought Roses battle was settled in the 34th minute when Leeds' defender David Wetherall rose above Gary Pallister and headed Gary Kelly's free-kick past Schmeichel.

ALLSPORT

Youth versus Experience: Danny Cadamarteri struggles with Nigel Winterburn

∧ In the meeting with leaders Arsenal at Goodison Park, Everton fans finally had something to cheer about after their miserable start to the season. With neighbours Liverpool bringing youngsters of the likes of Michael Owen through the ranks, the blue half of Merseyside rose to acclaim two 17-year-olds of their own in the 2–2 draw with the Londoners. Arsenal raced to a 2–0 lead at the interval with goals from Wright and Overmars but Everton fought back after the break. First, rookie defender Michael Ball headed in from close range and, seven minutes later, Goodison rose to greet a new hero when the dreadlocked Cadamarteri equalised from close range.

Youth and Experience: Gary Kelly leaves Paul Scholes on the deck as Leeds defeat the old enemy

ALLSPORT

1998 OCTOBER 5 – OCTOBER 18

Monday October 5 1998

Tuesday October 6 1998

Wednesday October 7 1998

Thursday October 8 1998

Friday October 9 1998

Saturday October 10 1998

Sunday October 11 1998

Monday October 12 1998

Tuesday October 13 1998

Wednesday October 14 1998

Thursday October 15 1998

Friday October 16 1998

Saturday October 17 1998
Charlton Athletic at Chelsea

Sunday October 18 1998

Manchester United had begun their Champions' League campaign with an impressive 3–0 victory away at FC Kosice, but Alex Ferguson knew the real test was to come. On 1 October Italian champions Juventus, European Cup finalists last season, winners the year before, arrived at Old Trafford in confident mood but were completely outplayed by a rampant United. In a stunning display of passing and movement, the champions of England put on their finest performance for years with goals from Sheringham, Scholes and Giggs securing the 3–1 win. Alex Ferguson even forgot to check his stopwatch.

ALLSPORT

Giggs... all set for another season of achievement

After leading Stockport County to promotion, manager Dave Jones found himself in demand with Premiership Southampton after Graeme Souness' acrimonious Saints walkout. But Jones soon found the Premiership going tough, and after 10 games, Southampton were rooted to the bottom of the table. And then West Ham visited the Dell on 4 October. Both teams huffed and puffed through the first half in front of a watching Glenn Hoddle, but the Saints broke the Hammers' resistance when substitute Ostenstad poked in from close range. Kevin Davies, the Saints' new signing from last season's FA Cup dream-merchants Chesterfield, extended the lead before Jason Dodd settled the issue with a 30-yard pile driver.

'Carlton, you're supposed to hold the ball up, not scorer Jason Dodd!'

ALLSPORT

Paul Ince, in Terry Butcher mould, looks on as Italy fail to score

ALLSPORT

11 October: England's trip to Rome for the World Cup showdown with Italy proved one of the most memorable nights in recent football history. Needing just a point to be sure of qualifying for France 98, England produced one of their most assured performances ever to secure a draw at the Olympic Stadium. With Newcastle's David Batty and Liverpool's Paul Ince outstanding in midfield, England soaked up the pressure and guaranteed their qualification. There was controversy, though, as the treatment meted out to travelling supporters by Italian police was universally deplored. 'The provocation the England fans had was unbelievable,' claimed England manager Glenn Hoddle, as the extent of the trouble was revealed in the aftermath.

The repercussions from the Rome game continued to resonate all week, only being taken off the back-page headline positions by Glenn Hoddle's shock divorce announcement. On the events in Rome, politicians from all hues of the political spectrum weighed in with their opinions, and David Mellor made the trip to Italy to confront Rome's chief of police on behalf of the BBC's Watchdog consumer programme. The major worry however was not for the fans but for England's World Cup 2006 final bid. With Euro 96 and its policing receiving praise from all over the world, but with memories of Hysel and Italia 90 still at the forefront of European minds, any bid from this side of the channel was anything but firm in the balance.

English fans... but this time the terrace terror was in uniform

ALLSPORT

Quiz 2 Referee Quiz

1 In the event of the crossbar being broken, or somehow moved from its position, and replacing it is not possible, the referee will:
- a) Allow another item such as a taut rope to be used as a replacement.
- b) Allow play to continue without a crossbar
- c) Abandon the game.

2 The minimum height for a corner flagpole is
- a) 1.5m
- b) .5m
- c) 1.75m

3 A goal is scored from a throw-in. Does the referee:
- a) Disallow it?
- b) Use his discretion?
- c) Allow the goal?

4 Only eight players appear for one side in a professional eleven-a-side game. Does the referee:
- a) Abandon the game?
- b) Allow the game to continue?
- c) Allow non-registered players to fill-in and continue the game?

5 An outfield player swaps positions with the goalkeeper without informing the referee. The ref notices while the ball is in play. Does he?
- a) Immediately send both players off?
- b) Allow play to continue and wait for a natural break?
- c) Immediately book both players?

6 The ref gives a direct free kick in your penalty area. One of your players kicks it back to the keeper who misses the ball completely. The ball goes into your own net! Does the referee:
- a) Order the free kick to be taken again?
- b) Award a goal to the opposition?
- c) Award a corner-kick to the opposition?

7 What is wrong with the picture at the top of a penalty shoot-out?
- a) The goalkeeper of the team taking the kick is in the centre circle with the rest of his teammates. Should he be standing on the 18-yard line?
- b) The goalkeeper has his arms raised when they should be still and by his side?
- c) The referee is in the penalty area causing a distraction when he should be standing on the 18-yard line.

8 There are three minutes left in a game when one manager decides to make a substitution. Two minutes later the ball goes out of play, it takes one minute to make the substitution. Does the referee:
- a) Blow the whistle for full-time when the player enters the field?
- b) Book the manager for time-wasting?
- c) Add time on for the substitution?

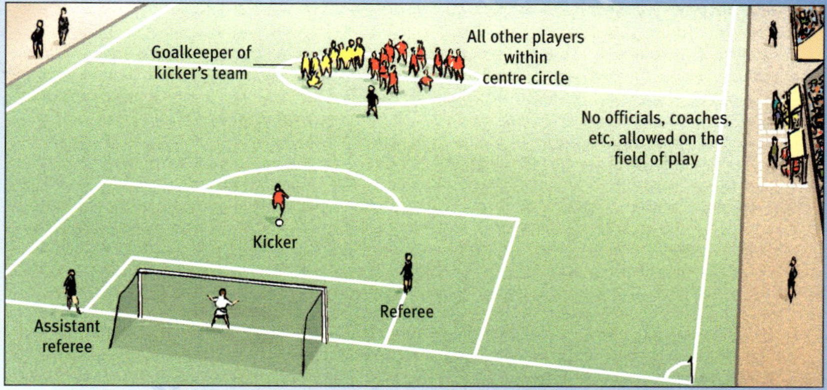

9 What is wrong with this picture of the 'Technical Area'?

- a) Nothing.
- b) There are no markings showing the correct distance.
- c) The distances shown are wrong.

10 In this picture, does the referee:
- a) Give the goal?
- b) Not give the goal?
- c) Give a drop-ball?

Answers: 1.c 2.a 3.a 4.b 5.b 6.c 7.a 8.c 9.a 10.b

Monday October 19 1998

Tuesday October 20 1998

Wednesday October 21 1998

Thursday October 22 1998

Friday October 23 1998

Saturday October 24 1998

Sunday October 25 1998
Chelsea at Leeds United

Monday October 26 1998

Tuesday October 27 1998

Wednesday October 28 1998

Thursday October 29 1998

Friday October 30 1998

Saturday October 31 1998
Aston Villa at Chelsea

Sunday November 1 1998

The Merseyside derby was as hotly contested as ever but it was the blue half of Liverpool who emerged victorious. Everton's 2–0 win on 18 October was capped by another fine display from new Goodison hero, 17-year-old Danny Cadamarteri and it relieved the pressure on beleaguered boss Howard Kendall. 'Liverpool are a quality side who make it difficult for you – now we need to maintain this standard,' said a delighted Kendall after the game. For Liverpool and Roy Evans, though, the defeat left them in mid-table and struggling to keep up the pace set by Arsenal and Manchester United.

ALLSPORT

Cadamarteri makes the Scouse Derby a day to remember for the Blues

Newcastle slumped to their biggest ever defeat under Kenny Dalglish when they went down 4–1 to Leeds at Elland Road. Leeds' recent run had seen them beat pace-setters Blackburn and Manchester United and they kept up their impressive form by racing to a 3–0 lead at the interval. Wetherall headed home just after the break to seal victory before Gillespie scored a late consolation for the visitors. 'It's the worst defeat by far since I came here and I hope it's just a blip, because we had no indication of this beforehand,' said a disappointed Dalglish.

Into the frying pan eh Kenny?
Dalglish tries to manage the Toon

ALLSPORT

Monday November 2 1998

Tuesday November 3 1998

Wednesday November 4 1998

Thursday November 5 1998

Friday November 6 1998

Saturday November 7 1998
Chelsea at West Ham United

Sunday November 8 1998

Monday November 9 1998

Tuesday November 10 1998

Wednesday November 11 1998

Thursday November 12 1998

Friday November 13 1998

Saturday November 14 1998
Wimbledon at Chelsea **FA Cup round 1**

Sunday November 15 1998

Chelsea survived a massive scare in their second-round European Cup Winners' Cup-tie against the battling Norwegians of Tromso on 23 October. The Blues were lucky to come away only 3–2 down, thanks to two late Gianluca Vialli goals, in a game played in blizzard conditions at a stadium some 200 miles inside the Arctic Circle. The referee stopped the tie three times so that ground staff could brush snow off the touchlines and penalty areas. 'We had to play into the blizzard, for 45 minutes, with the snow straight into our eyes so we couldn't see at all,' said a rueful then-manager Gullit after the game.

ALLSPORT

Andy Cole celebrating his hat-trick

Premier League champions Manchester United put Barnsley to the sword with a devastating display of finishing. Andy Cole rediscovered his goal touch with a supreme first-half hat-trick in a United display that had boss Alex Ferguson purring: 'Performances like that happen once or twice a season.' Barnsley fans, once famous for their 'it's just like watching Brazil' chant, were forced to change the lyrics to, 'it's just like watching Grange Hill'. But manager Danny Wilson remained ebullient after the game. 'There was nothing between the teams apart from seven goals,' he chirped.

The second-half blizzard in Tromso

ALLSPORT

Monday November 16 1998

Tuesday November 17 1998

Wednesday November 18 1998

Thursday November 19 1998

Friday November 20 1998

Saturday November 21 1998
Chelsea at Leicester City

Sunday November 22 1998

Monday November 23 1998

Tuesday November 24 1998

Wednesday November 25 1998

Thursday November 26 1998

Friday November 27 1998

Saturday November 28 1998
Sheffield Wednesday at Chelsea

Sunday November 29 1998

Coventry moved into a comfortable mid-table berth by beating Wimbledon 2–1 at Selhurst Park on 27 October. After narrowly escaping relegation on the last day of the previous season, Gordon Strachan's Sky Blues were aiming for loftier heights the following term. Goals from Darren Huckerby and Man of the Match Dion Dublin secured victory before a crowd of 11,201, the lowest Premiership gathering of the day. 'I must enjoy this job as I haven't taken to drink, my wife is still with me and there are not too many grey hairs,' said a delighted Strachan after the game.

ALLSPORT

Dion Dublin, surrounded by Light Blues, adds another goal to his tally

Promoted Bolton's first six matches at their new Reebok Stadium saw only three goals but no fewer than five sendings off. Stan Collymore, Alan Todd, Nathan Blake and Gary Pallister were all shown the red card (Pallister's was later quashed on appeal) before Robbie Fowler received his marching orders for elbowing Per Frandson. The dismissal crowned a mixed day for the England striker who had shot Liverpool into the lead in the first minute, before Blake pegged them back with an 84th minute equaliser. 'We all know if anyone raises their hands they have to go,' commented Bolton boss Colin Todd afterwards. And he should know.

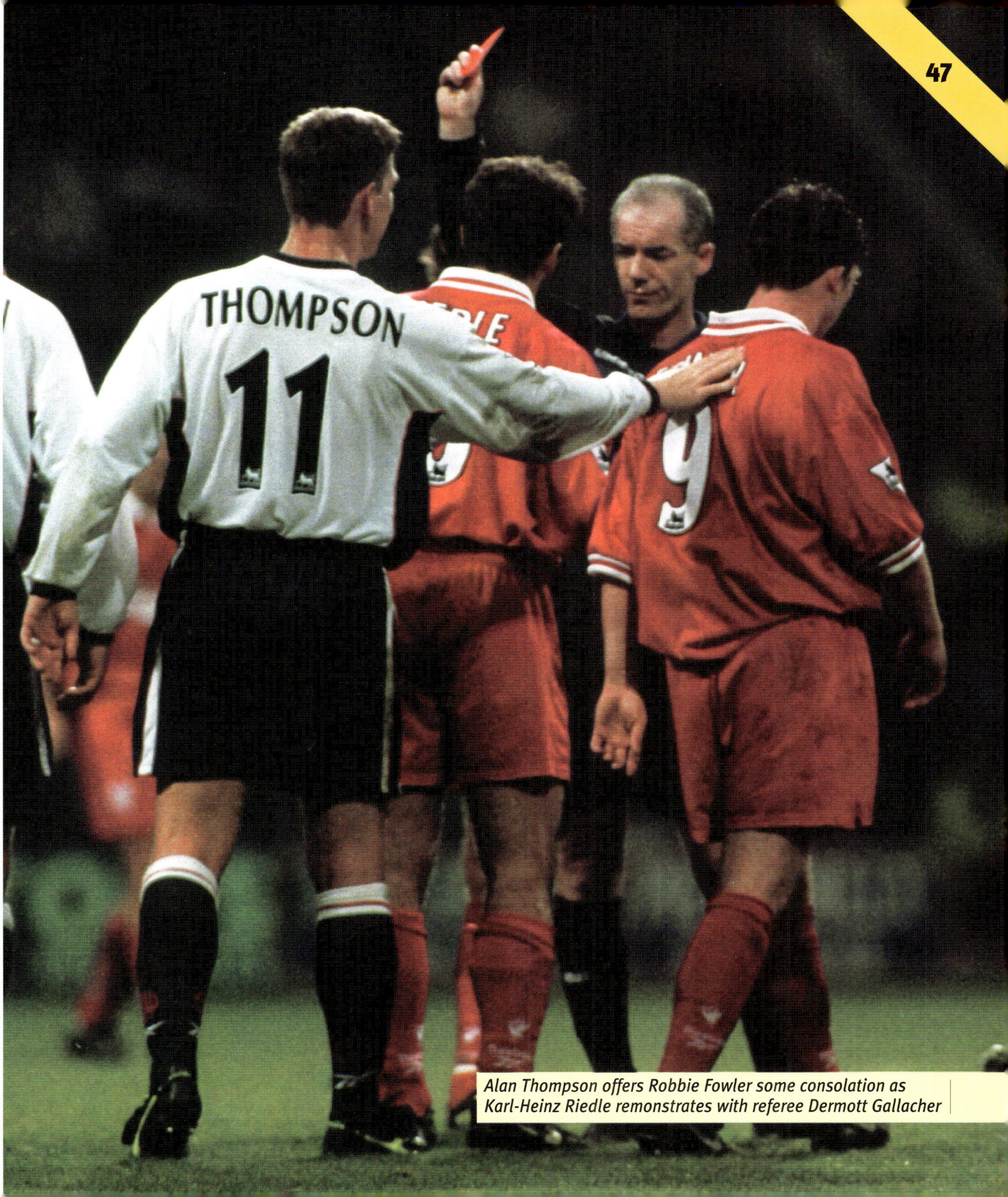

Alan Thompson offers Robbie Fowler some consolation as Karl-Heinz Riedle remonstrates with referee Dermott Gallacher

ALLSPORT

Monday November 30 1998

Tuesday December 1 1998

Wednesday December 2 1998

Thursday December 3 1998

Friday December 4 1998

Saturday December 5 1998
Chelsea at Everton **FA Cup round 2**

Sunday December 6 1998

Monday December 7 1998

Tuesday December 8 1998

Wednesday December 9 1998

Thursday December 10 1998

Friday December 11 1998

Saturday December 12 1998
Chelsea at Derby County

Sunday December 13 1998

Leeds produced an astonishing comeback to defeat Derby County 4–3 at Elland Road on 8 November. Substitutes Jimmy Floyd Hasselbaink and Lee Bowyer combined in the last minute and Bowyer rifled home the winner with a firm left-foot strike. This result would have been unthinkable after a first half-hour that saw Jim Smith's side race into a 3–0 lead. Dean Sturridge scored twice before Asanovic converted a spot-kick and the game looked all but over. But Leeds rallied and pulled back two goals before half-time. Then Hasselbaink converted a late penalty before Bowyer struck. George Graham was understandably pleased at the comeback. 'It just goes to show the camaraderie here. After the first 20 minutes I thought we were superb – the better team by far.'

ALLSPORT

Rodney Wallace adds to one of the most exciting Leeds versus Derby clashes in decades

Billed as the 'biggest Premiership game of the season so far,' Arsenal's 9 November attempt to close the gap on leaders Manchester United was not without incident. The Gunners marched into a 2–0 lead with impressive strikes from French duo Nicolas Anelka and Patrick Vieira before being pegged back before half-time by a brace from Teddy Sheringham. United then had a legitimate claim for a penalty refused by referee Martin Bodenham before Peter Schmeichel was hit by a missile thrown from the crowd. The perpetrator was later arrested. David Platt, in for the suspended Emmanuel Petit, secured the points for Arsenal with a flashing header, although most observers felt United's performance warranted at least a share of the points. Alex Ferguson later described the referee as 'a master of not seeing anything'.

Henning Berg discovers Peter Schmeichel's contact lenses in the game against Arsenal at Highbury

ALLSPORT

ALLSPORT

It's a Liverpool double as Steve MacManaman celebrates Robbie Fowler's first goal for England

England continued their build-up to World Cup France 98 with a comfortable 2–0 friendly victory over a poor Cameroon. The Africans were a pale shadow of the side that had performed so well on the world stage over the past few years. England's best player on the night was Manchester United striker Paul Scholes who capped an excellent performance with a superbly manufactured chip after great work from Paul Gascoigne. Minutes later, Robbie Fowler nodded home a David Beckham cross to make the game safe. Glenn Hoddle was gushing in his praise of Scholes afterwards: 'He could be the jewel in the crown because he can score goals and is proving it at club and international level.'

Leicester City's bright start to the season suffered a blip as they were beaten at Filbert Street by perennial party poopers Wimbledon on 15 November. The Dons registered in the 50th minute when Marcus Gayle's header was judged to have crossed the line after it hit the crossbar and rebounded out. It was all the more annoying for the Foxes because victory would have seen them leapfrog into the heady heights of 5th in the table, above the likes of Liverpool and Newcastle. But once again, Wimbledon confounded their critics, and their opposition, to steal the three points.

Right: Marcus Gayle beats Matt Eliot to the ball as the Dons hunt the Foxes

QUIZ 3 ABOUT CHELSEA

1 What was strange about Chelsea's 1966 Fairs Cup third round victory over AC Milan?
- a) It was played at Craven Cottage
- b) Chelsea won on the toss of a coin
- c) Milan won with only nine men on the field

2 What was the aggregate score when Chelsea met Jeunesse Hautcharage in the European Cup?
- a) 1–0
- b) 11–0
- c) 21–0

3 How long did it take Vinnie Jones to get sent off against Sheffield United in 1992?
- a) Two minutes, 11 seconds
- b) One minute, 33 seconds
- c) Three seconds

ALLSPORT

4 Which player holds the current Premiership for scoring in consecutive matches with seven?
- a) David Rocastle
- b) Mark Stein
- c) Gianfranco Zola

5 How many seconds did it take Roberto di Matteo to score the fastest FA Cup Final goal at Wembley in 1997?
- a) 52
- b) 42
- c) 32

6 How old was Jimmy Greaves when he scored his 100th League goal against Man City on 19 November, 1960
- a) 21 years, 248 days
- b) 20 years, 248 days
- c) 19 years, 248 days

7 Of whom did Ken Bates say, 'He has a strong wife, maybe I should have made her manager,' just after sacking him?
- a) Ian Porterfield
- b) Ruud Gullit
- c) John Hollins

8 How much did Ken Bates pay for Chelsea in 1982?
- a) £10 million
- b) £100
- c) £1

9 Who is Chelsea's most capped international?
- a) Jimmy Greaves
- b) Ray Wilkins
- c) Charlie Cook

10 What's the connection between Chelsea managers Ian Porterfield, Glen Hoddle and David Webb?
- a) They have all scored League Cup winners
- b) They have all scored UEFA Cup winners
- c) They have all scored FA Cup winners

Answers: 1.b 2.c 3.c 4.b 5.b 6.b 7.c 8.c 9.b 10.c

Monday December 14 1998

Tuesday December 15 1998

Wednesday December 16 1998
Chelsea at Manchester United

Thursday December 17 1998

Friday December 18 1998

Saturday December 19 1998
Tottenham Hotspur at Chelsea

Sunday December 20 1998

Monday December 21 1998

Tuesday December 22 1998

Wednesday December 23 1998

Thursday December 24 1998

Friday December 25 1998

Saturday December 26 1998
Chelsea at Southampton

Sunday December 27 1998

Barnsley sprung the Premiership's biggest upset of 1997 when they beat Liverpool 1–0 at Anfield on 22 November. Ashley Ward, out for the previous month suffering from viral meningitis, scored the game's only goal when Andy Liddell's cross bounced off Patrik Berger's shins allowing Ward to convert from close range. 'The boss asked me on Thursday if I wanted to play. To score at Liverpool of all places makes it complete,' said the delighted Barnsley striker. Liverpool had plenty of chances to equalise, with Karl-Heinz Riedle the main culprit. 'We did no defending,' was Roy Evans' stinging verdict.

ALLSPORT

'BFR' is back in the 'best job in the world' at Hillsborough

Ron Atkinson's return to club management with Sheffield Wednesday got off to a great start with a fine 2–0 victory over Premiership frontrunners Arsenal. In his previous managerial stint at Wednesday, Atkinson delivered the Owls' first major trophy in 56 years when they lifted the League Cup. It ended in acrimony when 'Big' Ron left to manage Aston Villa. But all was forgotten as Sheffield Wednesday's biggest crowd of the season to date, 34,373, turned up to see Arsene Wenger's Arsenal comfortably beaten. Goals from Andy Booth and Guy Whittingham sealed Wednesday's victory and Atkinson was understandably jubilant. 'I can see real quality in this team,' he said afterwards.

ALLSPORT

Barnsley pull a famous away victory out of the bag with an Ashley Ward goal

Monday December 28 1998

Tuesday December 29 1998
Manchester United at Chelsea

Wednesday December 30 1998

Thursday December 31 1998

Friday January 1 1999

Saturday January 2 1999
FA Cup round 3

Sunday January 3 1999

Monday January 4 1999

Tuesday January 5 1999

Wednesday January 6 1999

Thursday January 7 1999

Friday January 8 1999

Saturday January 9 1999
Chelsea at Newcastle United

Sunday January 10 1999

29 November: Goals from Ramon Vega and David Ginola provided Tottenham's new manager Christian Gross with the perfect start and sank beleaguered Everton further into the relegation mire. Hundreds of fans remained in the Goodison stands after the match to call for the Toffees' chairman, Peter Johnson, to relinquish control of the club. And the defeat sent Everton to rock bottom in the Premiership table. Swiss star Vega opened the scoring in the 72nd minute, nodding home an Andy Sinton cross after Ruel Fox had flicked the ball on. Then David Ginola ran the Everton defence ragged before firing past Southall with a decisive left foot strike.

ALLSPORT

Christian Gross hops from Grasshoppers to Spurs

30 November: Manchester United comprehensively outplayed second-placed Blackburn to stretch their lead at the top of the Premiership. A brace from Ole Solskjaer and own-goals from Stefan Henchoz and Jeff Kenna left the chasing pack in no doubt as to the task they faced in toppling the champions. Solskjaer opened the scoring in the 18th minute, neatly chesting the ball down before converting from close range. And early in the second half, the Norwegian outpaced the Rovers' defence to power in a right-foot strike from the edge of the area. To compound Blackburn's misery, England forward Chris Sutton was sent from the field of play after lunging at Nicky Butt.

Baby-faced he may be, but Ole Gunnar Solskjaer showed immense early maturity for Manchester United

ALLSPORT

Monday January 11 1999

Tuesday January 12 1999

Wednesday January 13 1999

Thursday January 14 1999

Friday January 15 1999

Saturday January 16 1999
Coventry City at Chelsea

Sunday January 17 1999

Monday January 18 1999

Tuesday January 19 1999

Wednesday January 20 1999

Thursday January 21 1999

Friday January 22 1999

Saturday January 23 1999
FA Cup round 4

Sunday January 24 1999

V Andy Cole struck twice to settle Manchester United's Saturday morning, 6 December, showdown with bitter rivals Liverpool at Anfield. The in-form United striker opened his account early in the second half after a mistake by Bjorn Kvarme. But Liverpool equalised nine minutes later after Nicky Butt clattered Michael Owen in the box – Robbie Fowler converted the spot-kick. However, the Premiership leaders were not to be denied. David Beckham struck a beautiful 22-yard free-kick over the Liverpool wall and past David James, and then Cole settled the issue, slotting home neatly from close range. 'We won't give up but, realistically, our best bet for honours is now in the cups,' said a disappointed Roy Evans afterwards.

ALLSPORT

Andy Cole's second goal against Liverpool

> Tottenham's second match under the stewardship of Christian Gross ended in their heaviest home defeat since 1935. Ruud Gullit's Chelsea struck six times, with five goals coming after the break. Norwegian striker Tor Andre Flo helped himself to a hat-trick, the third a delightful chip over Spurs keeper Ian Walker. 'That was the easiest match I have experienced in English football,' said the delighted Flo. 'I was surprised how Spurs collapsed after our second goal.' But it was back to the drawing board for former Grasshoppers Zurich manager Gross.

Chelsea's team spirit builds yet again as Tor Andre Flo is buried under an international bundle

ALLSPORT

Monday January 25 1999

Tuesday January 26 1999

Wednesday January 27 1999

Thursday January 28 1999

Friday January 29 1999

Saturday January 30 1999

Chelsea at Arsenal

Sunday January 31 1999

Monday February 1 1999

Tuesday February 2 1999

Wednesday February 3 1999

Thursday February 4 1999

Friday February 5 1999

Saturday February 6 1999

Southampton at Chelsea

Sunday February 7 1999

On 13 December, Barnsley's former Newcastle hitman John Hendrie rescued a welcome point for the Yorkshiremen against Kenny Dalglish's side. Hendrie fired home a 20-yard bullet past Shaka Hislop in the 75th minute after two goals from Newcastle winger Keith Gillespie had looked like keeping up Newcastle's faltering Premiership challenge. Barnsley took the lead in the ninth minute when Neil Redfearn curled the ball into the top corner, before Gillespie struck twice, either side of half-time. 'There's been an all-round improvement,' said the relieved Barnsley boss Danny Wilson afterwards. 'I think we're learning.'

ALLSPORT

Ian Walker, Spurs' high-flying keeper...

Tottenham Hotspur's majestic Frenchman David Ginola lifted the gloom at White Hart Lane as Spurs coasted to a 3–0 victory over Danny Wilson's Barnsley on 20 December. Ginola capped a wonderful first-half display with two goals as Spurs raced to a three-goal lead in the first 18 minutes. Allen Nielson opened the scoring in the sixth minute when he latched onto a through-ball from Darren Anderton before dispatching a low drive past Lars Leese. But it was Ginola who basked in the limelight, orchestrating everything from the centre of Spurs' midfield. But once again, Danny Wilson was left lamenting his back line. 'We shot ourselves in the foot by making schoolboy errors,' he said afterwards.

Pistone of Newcastle bears down on Barnsley's Nicky Eaden

ALLSPORT

ALLSPORT

John Newsome looks on as Vialli shows the commitment for which he is rightfully known

20 December: Ron Atkinson's new Sheffield Wednesday charges were hammered 4–1 at Hillsborough by high-flying Chelsea's foreign legion. Goals by Dan Petrescu, Vialli, Flo and a converted spot-kick from Frank Leboeuf ensured that Ruud Gullit's side took the spoils. Romanian Petrescu converted from just inside the 18-yard area in the 30th minute, and by the time Pembridge opened Wednesday's account, Chelsea had added two more. The best goal of the game was scored by Norwegian striker Tore Andre Flo when he swaggered through the Sheffield defence before firing past Pressman. 'I'm sure Chelsea have had harder practice matches than that,' fumed Big Ron after Wednesday's abject surrender.

Premiership leaders Manchester United overcame Howard Kendall's Everton with embarrassing ease at Old Trafford on Boxing Day. United hardly left first gear in a 2–0 victory which extended their run of consecutive league victories to six and afforded them a six-point gap at the Premiership summit. Henning Berg opened United's account in the 14th minute, converting from close range after David Beckham's cross was headed back across goal by Ronny Johnson. And then Andy Cole fashioned a superb second, chipping Everton keeper Thomas Myhre from 25 yards. 'It was an embarrassing 90 minutes for us. It was men against boys and the scoreline flatters us,' said a dejected Howard Kendall afterwards.

Quiz 4 About The Premier League

1 Who won the first ever Premiership title?
a) Leeds United
b) Blackburn Rovers
c) Manchester United

2 Who holds the record for the least number of points accumulated in a Premiership season?
a) Swindon Town
b) Ipswich Town
c) Bolton Wanderers

3 Who was the Premiership top scorer in the 1993-94 season?
a) Alan Shearer
b) Andy Cole
c) Teddy Sheringham

4 Who was footballer of the year that same season?
a) Alan Shearer
b) Andy Coal
c) Teddy Sheringham

Manchester United's Nicky Butt eye on the ball... and the prize

ALLSPORT

5 In which stadium did Blackburn Rovers clinch the 1994-95 title?
a) Upton Park
b) Ewood Park
c) Anfield

6 During which Premiership season was Arsenal manager George Graham banned from football for a year for receiving 'bungs'?
a) 1993-94
b) 1994-95
c) 1995-96

7 Which Premiership club were Manchester United playing in April 1996 when they famously abandoned their grey kit at half-time?
a) Coventry City
b) Southampton
c) Sheffield Wednesday

8 Which company signed a deal to sponsor the Premiership in February 1993?
a) Carling
b) Littlewoods
c) Bass

9 Which foreign star scored a hat-trick on his Premiership debut in 1996?
a) Patrick Berger
b) Gianfranco Zola
c) Fabrizio Ravanelli

10 Who was the first player to score a hat-trick in the Premiership?
a) Alan Shearer
b) Eric Cantona
c) Ian Wright

Answers: 1.c 2.b 3.a 4.a 5.c 6.c 7.b 8.c 9.c 10.b

Monday February 8 1999

Tuesday February 9 1999

Wednesday February 10 1999

Thursday February 11 1999

Friday February 12 1999

Saturday February 13 1999
Blackburn Rovers at Chelsea **FA Cup round 5**

Sunday February 14 1999

Monday February 15 1999

Tuesday February 16 1999

Wednesday February 17 1999

Thursday February 18 1999

Friday February 19 1999

Saturday February 20 1999
Chelsea at Nottingham Forest

Sunday February 21 1999

Tottenham and Arsenal shared the spoils in the North London derby at White Hart Lane on 28 December. But the draw left Spurs languishing in the relegation zone with fellow strugglers Barnsley and Everton. The majority of the 29,000 faithful were hoping that Jürgen Klinsmann could score the goal to sink Arsene Wenger's Gunners. And although the Germany captain didn't oblige, he did have a hand in Spurs' opener. In the 28th minute, Ruel Fox crossed from the right, Klinsmann flicked on and Allan Nielson converted smartly from close range. But Arsenal were not to be denied a share of the points. On the hour, Ray Parlour struck from just inside the box, his shot deflecting off Ramon Vega past Walker. 'Tottenham were really pumped up,' commented Arsene Wenger afterwards. 'Their determination really surprised in the first 30 minutes.'

ALLSPORT

Paul Ince – close marking is no longer a problem

3 January 1998, and Liverpool slumped to an embarrassing home defeat at the first hurdle in the FA Cup against Coventry. The Reds were booed off the park by the Anfield faithful after Gordon Strachan's impressive Coventry had burst through Liverpool's leaky rearguard almost at will. Roy Evans could not have imagined such a reverse when Jamie Rednapp's free-kick curled around the wall and into the net in the seventh minute. But on the stroke of half-time, Darren Huckerby cut a swathe through the Liverpool defence before slotting home from an acute angle. Dion Dublin added another midway through the second half before Paul Telfer ensured Coventry would be in the bag for the fourth round.

Klinsmann's shock return to White Hart Lane was yet another attempt to lift Spurs' nose-diving season

ALLSPORT

Monday February 22 1999

Tuesday February 23 1999

Wednesday February 24 1999

Thursday February 25 1999

Friday February 26 1999

Saturday February 27 1999
Liverpool at Chelsea

Sunday February 28 1999

Monday March 1 1999

Tuesday March 2 1999

Wednesday March 3 1999

Thursday March 4 1999

Friday March 5 1999

Saturday March 6 1999
Chelsea at Middlesbrough **FA Cup quarter-finals**

Sunday March 7 1999

Unibond League part-timers Emley almost pulled off a sensational result against West Ham on 3 January. The Yorkshire village side (population 1,800), whose numbers include the obligatory fireman and postman, rocked the Premiership outfit with a battling display against the odds. And their moment of glory came 11 minutes into the second half when chemical plant worker Paul David headed home, to equalise Frank Lampard's fourth-minute opener. The non-leaguers were just nine minutes from forcing a replay when John Hartson nodded home from close range to seal victory. 'We have murdered Newcastle and Aston Villa here, but Emley gave us a much rougher ride,' said relieved England defender Rio Ferdinand afterwards.

ALLSPORT

Not quite a hat-trick for Giggs, but it kept Spurs well in check

10 January: Ryan Giggs capped a fine individual performance by scoring a brace against a Tottenham side boasting the recently returned German striker Jürgen Klinsmann. Alex Ferguson rested Nicky Butt, moved Paul Scholes to central midfield and gave Ole Solskjaer an outing on the left wing, but these changes made no difference to Manchester United's fluid rhythm. Giggs opened the scoring just before half-time with a solid drive from close range after Spurs keeper Baardson failed to hold a Beckham cross. The Welshman headed home another Beckham centre after the break to extend United's lead at the top of the Premiership.

Rio Ferdinand, the West Ham youth finally got to play for England after a drive-in with the law

ALLSPORT

Monday March 8 1999

Tuesday March 9 1999

Wednesday March 10 1999

Thursday March 11 1999

Friday March 12 1999

Saturday March 13 1999
West Ham United at Chelsea

Sunday March 14 1999

Monday March 15 1999

Tuesday March 16 1999

Wednesday March 17 1999

Thursday March 18 1999

Friday March 19 1999

Saturday March 20 1999
Chelsea at Aston Villa

Sunday March 21 1999

Vauxhall Conference side Stevenage Borough almost pulled off a sensational FA Cup result against Premiership giants Newcastle on 24 January. The hullabaloo surrounding Stevenage's right to stage the game at Broadhall Way failed to take the edge off a hard fought cup tie, as the Vauxhall Conference side bravely fought out a 1–1 draw. But it looked bleak for Stevenage as early as the third minute when Alan Shearer comfortably headed home Keith Gillespie's cross. It was the England striker's first goal since his return from six months on the sidelines. But the Conference side took the game to Newcastle for the remainder of the half, Guiliano Grazioli's close-range strike just reward for their efforts.

ALLSPORT

Another goal for the Cottee family scrapbook

On 31 January, Leicester City caused one of the shocks of the season when they defeated champions Manchester United 1–0 at Old Trafford, thus ending United's unbeaten home record. Leicester's veteran striker Tony Cottee latched onto a Garry Parker through ball in the 20th minute and slid the ball past Peter Schmeichel from close range. Cottee, famous for logging every goal in his personal scrapbook, was only in the side because Ian Marshall was out injured. 'We got what we deserved,' commented a rueful Alex Ferguson afterwards. 'We were too casual, particularly in the first half.'

Guiliano Grazioli's giant-stalling, if not killing, goal took the gingerbread off Newcastle's day

ALLSPORT

Monday March 22 1999

Tuesday March 23 1999

Wednesday March 24 1999

Thursday March 25 1999

Friday March 26 1999

Saturday March 27 1999

Sunday March 28 1999

Monday March 29 1999

Tuesday March 30 1999

Wednesday March 31 1999

Thursday April 1 1999

Friday April 2 1999

Saturday April 3 1999
Chelsea at Charlton Athletic

Sunday April 4 1999

V Struggling Tottenham Hotspur upset the form book with an amazing 3–0 victory away at Blackburn Rovers on 7 February. Christian Gross, Spurs' Swiss manager had had little to shout about in his unsteady reign until this decisive victory at Ewood Park. Nicola Berti, Tottenham's midfield signing from Inter Milan, opened the scoring on 37 minutes, knocking the ball past Tim Flowers from close range. But although the majority of chances fell to Blackburn, Spurs extended their lead in the last minute when substitute Chris Armstrong struck a low drive from the edge of the box before Ruel Fox made the points safe in injury time. 'A lot has been said about Tottenham but we showed what we can do,' said a relieved Chris Armstrong, after three months out injured.

ALLSPORT

Sol Campbell makes life interesting for Blackburn's Damien Duff

➤ A resurgent Arsenal overcame Chelsea 2–0 in a hard fought London derby at Highbury the next day. Two first-half goals from the Gunners' 21-year-old midfield sensation Stephen Hughes settled the issue, and earned him a new contract in the process. As early as the fourth minute, Nicolas Anelka latched onto a careless back pass by Frank Leboeuf, only to see his shot well saved by Ed de Goey. But the ball rebounded back into the area and Hughes slammed home an unstoppable left-foot shot from 16 yards. And just before half-time, Hughes was the first to react after Chelsea failed to clear a corner kick, the youngster nodding home inside the six-yard box. Little did Chelsea boss Ruud Gullit know he would get the sack a week later.

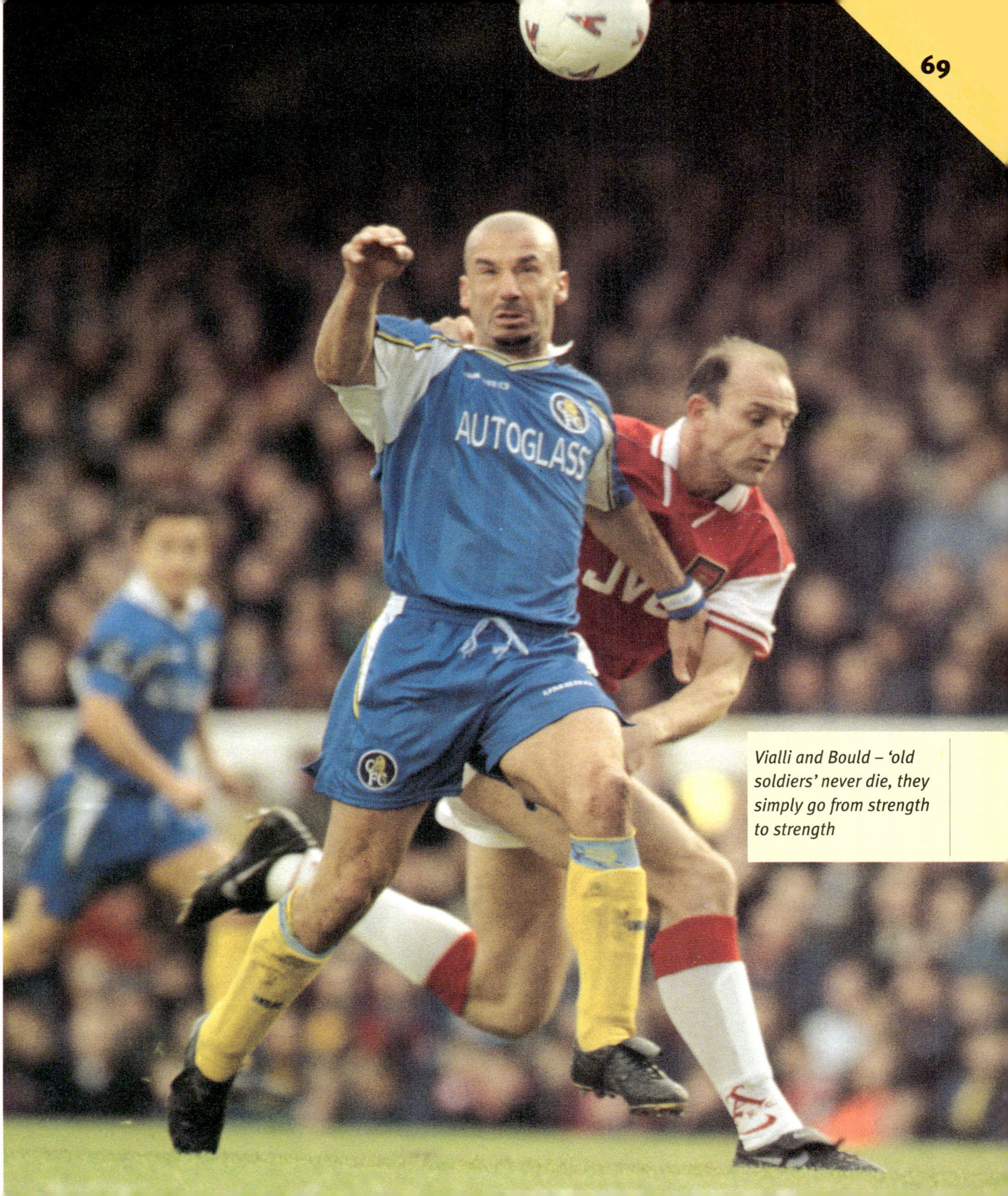

Vialli and Bould – 'old soldiers' never die, they simply go from strength to strength

Liverpool's precocious teenage striker Michael Owen capped the finest week of his career with a first senior hat-trick against Sheffield Wednesday at Hillsborough. The youngster, crowned 'Man of the Match' in England's 2–0 reverse against Chile at Wembley just three days previously, helped Liverpool salvage a point after they had trailed 3–1. Goals by Di Canio, Carbone and Andy Hinchcliffe looked set to secure victory for Ron Atkinson's Wednesday but it was Owen who took centre stage with two stunning late goals. 'Michael's frightening,' said Kevin Pressman, after Owen's devasting trio. 'Every keeper in the world will – believe me – worry about him.'

Paul Ince with his shooting boots on bemuses the Sheffield Wednesday defence yet again

Club-record signing Viorel Moldovan fired Coventry City into the last eight of the FA Cup against Aston Villa on Valentine's Day. The £3.25 million Romanian striker came off the bench to send Coventry's fans into Sky Blue heaven – it was their first victory at Villa Park after 25 unsuccessful attempts. Gordon Strachan's side were the better team throughout and deserved their victory over a lacklustre Villa, whose only genuine moment of class came after keeper Mark Bosnich pulled off a remarkable reflex save, volleying away Soltvedt's strike on goal. 'The winning goal was not just about getting into the last eight of the FA Cup, it was a claim for a first team place,' said a determined Moldovan afterwards.

Mark Bosnich dives to stop Moldovan's shot

Quiz 5 Referee Quiz

1 According to FIFA, what is the minimum length of a pitch used in an international game?

a) 90 metres
b) 95 metres
c) 100 metres

2 What is the acceptable pressure of a football?

a) 0.6 to 1.1 atmospheres
b) 0.5 to 1.25 atmospheres
c) 0.75 to 2 atmospheres

3 Is the red attacking number 10 offside in this Diagram?

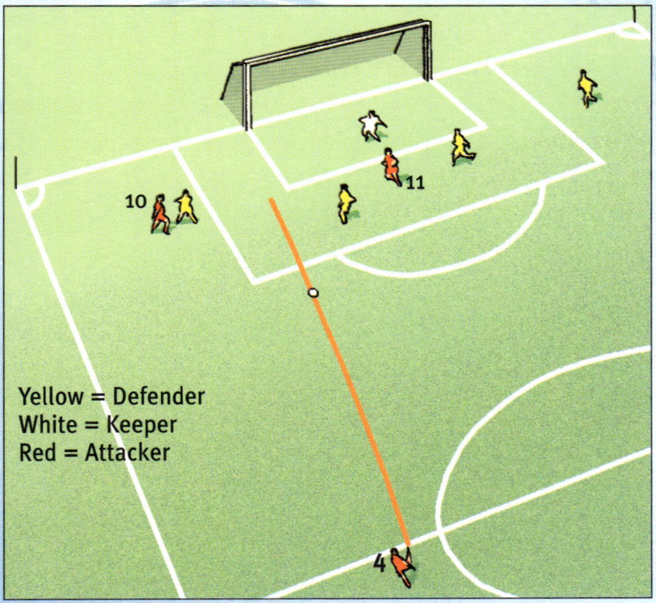

a) No
b) Yes
c) Yes, but he's not interfering with play

4 When needs to go to penalties, who decides which end they are to be taken from?

a) A toss of a coin before the game begins
b) The referee decides
c) A toss of a coin before the penalties are taken

5 If, during a penalty shoot-out, the keeper is injured and all substitutes have been used already, who replaces the keeper?

a) A substitute keeper
b) No one
c) One of the outfield players

6 Your free-kick specialist takes a corner by flicking the ball in the air and curling it into the goal. What does the referee do?

a) Awards the goal as fair
b) Awards an indirect free-kick to the opposition (the corner taker is only allowed to touch the ball once until another player touches it).
c) Awards a direct free-kick to the opposition (the corner taker is only allowed to touch the ball once until another player touches it).

7 Your keeper takes a free-kick but trips and the ball doesn't make it out of the area. What should the ref do?

a) Has it taken again
b) Allows play to continue
c) Awards an indirect free-kick to the opposition

8 An opposition player persistently stands nose-to-nose with one of your team who is trying to take a throw-in, what should the referee do?

a) Get the opposition player to stand 10-yards back
b) Award an indirect free-kick to your team
c) Caution the opposition player and give him a yellow card

9 What is the referee awarding in this Diagram?

a) An indirect free-kick
b) A corner
c) A direct free-kick

10 If an indirect free-kick goes straight into the goal, what should the referee do?

a) Have the kick re-taken
b) Award an indirect free-kick to the opposition
c) Award a goal kick

Answers: 1.c 2.a 3.a 4.b 5.c 6.b 7.a 8.c 9.a 10.c

Monday April 5 1999
Leeds United at Chelsea

Tuesday April 6 1999

Wednesday April 7 1999

Thursday April 8 1999

Friday April 9 1999

Saturday April 10 1999
Chelsea at Wimbledon

FA Cup semi-finals

Sunday April 11 1999

Monday April 12 1999

Tuesday April 13 1999

Wednesday April 14 1999

Thursday April 15 1999

Friday April 16 1999

Saturday April 17 1999
Leicester City at Chelsea

Sunday April 18 1999

Coventry condemned Danny Wilson's Barnsley to another cruel Premiership defeat on 21 February. Dion Dublin settled the issue in the 89th minute, converting a controversial spot-kick after he had been challenged in the 18 yard area by Peter Markstedt. Although Barnsley felt hard done by the decision, both Darren Huckerby and George Boateng had chances to settle the issue long before the penalty was awarded. Dublin's 17th goal of the campaign left his manager Gordon Strachan in a quandary about where to play him. 'Dion wants to be a forward because there's nothing like scoring goals, but in the long term centre-half may be his best position,' said the Sky Blues' boss.

ALLSPORT

Patrick Vieira – strength, skill and style in an Arsenal shirt

The same day, Wimbledon outfought a disappointing Aston Villa side at Selhurst Park to move above Brian Little's men in the Premiership. Jason Euell opened the scoring in the 10th minute and Carl Leaburn extended the Dons' lead half an hour later, heading home neatly in the six-yard box. Although Savo Milosevic pulled a goal back on the stroke of half-time, any hope Villa had of rescuing a point disappeared when he limped off shortly after the break. 'There is no point in sitting down and feeling sorry for ourselves – we have just got to get on with it,' said Villa skipper Gareth Southgate afterwards. But for beleagured boss Brian Little, it was one defeat too many. He resigned just days later.

Stan-the-Man out-leaps Wimbledon's Jones and Perry, can he see Brian Little leaving by the side entrance?

ALLSPORT

Monday April 19 1999

Tuesday April 20 1999

Wednesday April 21 1999

Thursday April 22 1999

Friday April 23 1999

Saturday April 24 1999

Chelsea at Sheffield Wednesday

Sunday April 25 1999

Monday April 26 1999

Tuesday April 27 1999

Wednesday April 28 1999

Thursday April 29 1999

Friday April 30 1999

Saturday May 1 1999

Everton at Chelsea

Sunday May 2 1999

Manchester United returned to the scene of their emphatic FA Cup victory to inflict another defeat over Chelsea at Stamford Bridge on 28 February. And United's winner came from an unlikely source. In the 31st minute, Philip Neville, playing on unfamiliar territory on the right side of midfield, popped up to slot the ball neatly past Dmitri Kharine. The Blues' player boss Gianluca Vialli, in only his third game at the helm, failed to lift Chelsea despite his presence on the field from the start. But he was full of praise for Ferguson's side afterwards. 'On the counter attack they are like the great European sides,' he enthused. 'One minute you are in their area, the next they break out and score.'

ALLSPORT

England versus Italy as Philip Neville battles with Roberto de Matteo in Manchester United's demolition of Chelsea at Stamford Bridge

Chris Sutton scored a sparkling hat-trick against Leicester City at Ewood Park to remind Glenn Hoddle of his World Cup credentials. Sutton, who had refused to play for the England B team after being omitted from the senior squad, struck twice in the first half and completed his hat-trick soon after half-time with a superb chip over Kasey Keller. Leicester scored three late goals but Rovers held on for the points. 'You don't have to be a genius to work out that I haven't done my chances any good,' said Sutton after the game. 'But I believe in what I did and that's just as important to me.'

Chris Sutton's claim to the ball is stronger than his claim to an England place now

ALLSPORT

Monday May 3 1999

Tuesday May 4 1999

Wednesday May 5 1999

Thursday May 6 1999

Friday May 7 1999

Saturday May 8 1999
Chelsea at Tottenham Hotspur

Sunday May 9 1999

Monday May 10 1999

Tuesday May 11 1999

Wednesday May 12 1999

Thursday May 13 1999

Friday May 14 1999

Saturday May 15 1999

Sunday May 16 1999
Derby County at Chelsea

14 March: Manchester United's slump in form continued when Arsenal arrived at Old Trafford for an 11.15 a.m. kick-off and deservedly left with the three points. Marc Overmars' goal in the 79th minute stunned the majority of the 55,174 into silence. The diminutive Dutch winger had been a constant menace to United's defence throughout and he outpaced Gary Neville to slot home under Schmeichel after Patrick Vieira had headed the ball into his path. And for the first time in weeks, the Premiership title was no longer in the hands of the champions. 'We're now looking to win seven league matches in a row which is what we're capable of doing if we get key players back,' said Alex Ferguson afterwards.

ALLSPORT

Bergkamp keeps his eyes on the prize as Man United crash at home

Leeds United put in their most impressive performance of the season to date with a stunning 5–0 victory against Derby at Pride Park on 15 March. It was the first time the Rams had conceded more than two goals at their new stadium and George Graham's men cut Derby's defence to shreds with a fine counter-attacking performance. Leeds were 3–0 to the good by half-time with goals from Gunnar Halle, Lee Bowyer and an own-goal from Derby defender Jacob Larsen. Kewell and Hasselbaink converted smartly after the interval to leave their delighted manager singing the praises of his team. 'We played some great football with a lot of style,' said Graham after the game.

Gunnar Halle looks on as Leeds slot another in their 5–0 demolition of Derby at Pride Park

ALLSPORT

1999 MAY 17 – MAY 30

Monday May 17 1999

Tuesday May 18 1999

Wednesday May 19 1999

Thursday May 20 1999

Friday May 21 1999

Saturday May 22 1999
FA Cup Final

Sunday May 23 1999

Monday May 24 1999

Tuesday May 25 1999

Wednesday May 26 1999

Thursday May 27 1999

Friday May 28 1999

Saturday May 29 1999

Sunday May 30 1999

On 17 March Alan Kelly pulled off three spectacular saves in a tense penalty shootout against Coventry City to send Sheffield United into the semi-finals of the FA Cup. Republic of Ireland keeper Kelly saved spot-kicks from Dion Dublin, David Burrows and Simon Hayworth, but it was the Blades who were grateful that the game went into extra time. Coventry's Paul Telfer opened the scoring in the 10th minute as Gordon Strachan's men dominated the first half hour. United pressed for an equaliser, but they had to wait until the 89th minute, when the Sky Blues failed to clear a corner and skipper David Holdsworth banged in a volley from 12 yards.

ALLSPORT

Darren Huckerby does his best to get Coventry to Wembley

Arsenal defeated London neighbours West Ham in a dramatic penalty shootout to send the Gunners through to an FA Cup semi-final meeting with Wolves. Tony Adams' spot-kick settled the issue, but Arsenal had to play over half the game without PFA Player of the Year Dennis Bergkamp. The Dutch striker was sent off by referee Mike Reed after he elbowed Hammers skipper Steve Lomas, Bergkamp's second dismissal of the season. Nicolas Anelka struck at the end of the first period to give Arsenal the lead before former Gunners' striker John Hartson equalised six minutes from the end. Five spot-kicks were missed in the penalty shootout but Tony Adams kept his nerve to fire past Bernard Lamas. It was a bad week for Arsenal's Premiership rivals Manchester United who crashed out of the European Cup to Monaco.

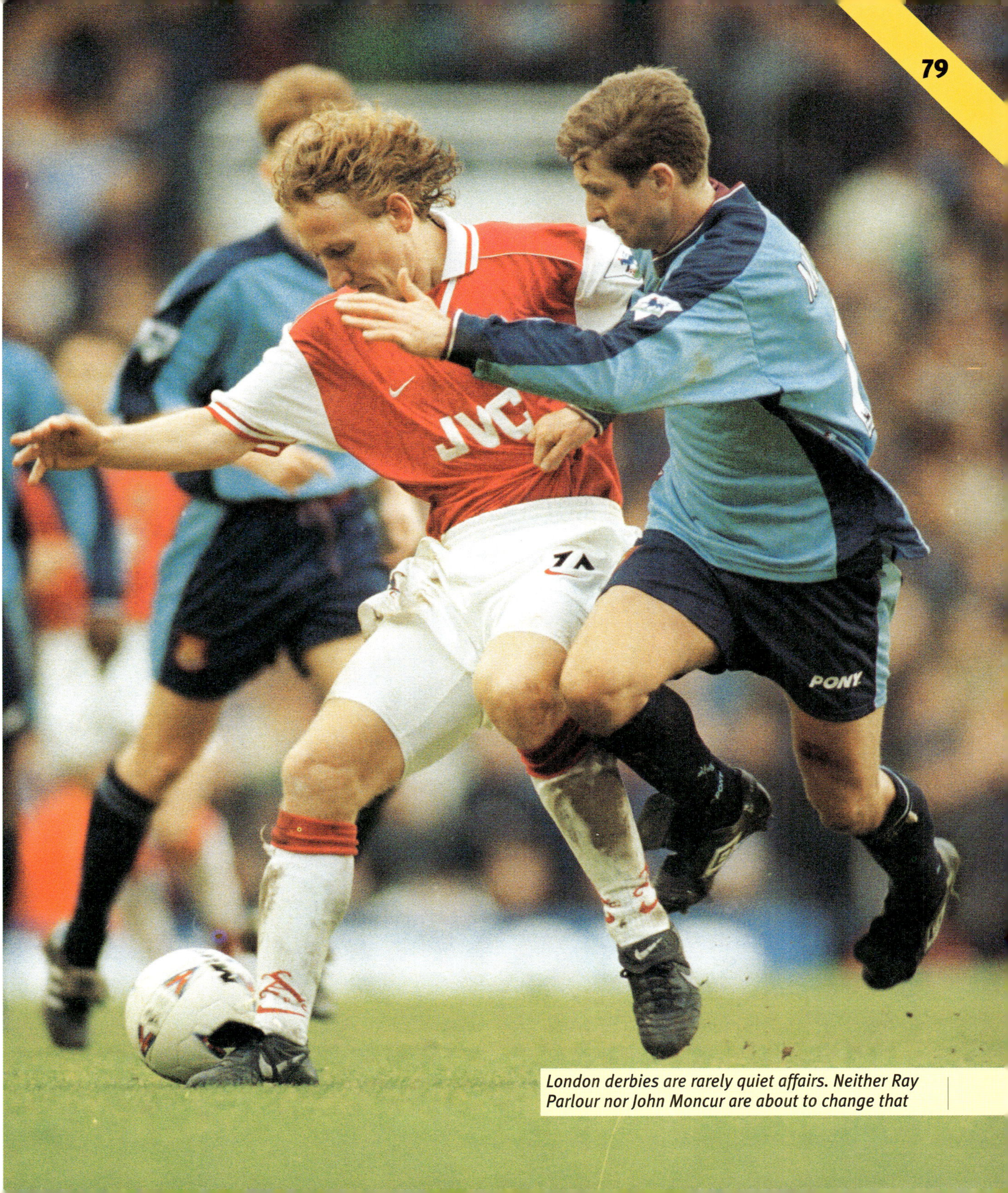

London derbies are rarely quiet affairs. Neither Ray Parlour nor John Moncur are about to change that

ALLSPORT

ALLSPORT

According to Barnsley, the referee hadn't learned the script properly, but the players certainly acted their parts in a resoundingly good argument

Referee Gary Willard sent off three Barnsley players in an explosive encounter against Liverpool at Oakwell on 28 March. At one stage, the proceedings became so heated that the Worthing official and his assistants had to leave the field with a police escort after irate Barnsley fans ran onto the pitch. A brace each from Barnsley skipper Neil Redfearn and Karl-Heinz Riedle suggested that the teams would share the spoils, only for Steve MacManaman to slot home from close range in the final minute to give Liverpool three points. However, it was the sendings off that made the headlines. 'The referee lost the plot, it's as simple as that,' said irate Barnsley boss Danny Wilson.

Chelsea player-manager Gianluca Vialli left himself out of his Coca-Cola Cup Final squad but ended up lifting the trophy. Two goals in extra time broke the stalemate and left Bryan Robson's Middlesbrough bridesmaids yet again. It was Boro's third Wembley defeat in 12 months. But it was a great day for Vialli, who preferred Mark Hughes and Tore Andre Flo to himself, and the victory came only weeks after the sensational departure of Ruud Gullit. Frank Sinclair opened the scoring in the first half of extra time before Roberto Di Matteo settled the issue. And Paul Gascoigne's Middlesbrough debut could easily have ended with his sending off. He was booked for a scything challenge on Zola and later made bad tackles on Hughes and Wise.

Quiz 6 About the Premier League

1 Which of the following clubs has not won the Premiership?
a) Liverpool
b) Blackburn Rovers
c) Leeds United

2 Who finished bottom of the Premiership after the 1996-97 season?
a) Nottingham Forest
b) Middlesbrough
c) Sunderland

3 Who was Young Player of the Year in 1994?
a) Andy Cole
b) David Beckham
c) Robbie Fowler

It could have been Ruud's, but Vialli's happy with the Coca-Cola Cup

ALLSPORT

4 Who has scored the fastest hat-trick in Premiership history?
a) Dion Dublin
b) Robbie Fowler
c) Alan Shearer

5 Which was the first ever Premiership season?
a) 1990-91
b) 1991-92
c) 1992-93

6 What was the first Premiership game to be broadcast on satellite television?
a) Nottingham Forest v Liverpool
b) Arsenal v Manchester United
c) Tottenham v Chelsea

7 Which club holds the record for the number of goals conceded in a Premiership season?
a) Swindon Town
b) Middlesbrough
c) Nottingham Forest

8 Which two clubs share the record for the fewest number of goals conceded in a Premiership season?
a) Arsenal and Leeds United
b) Arsenal and Blackburn Rovers
c) Arsenal and Manchester United

9 Which of the following Premiership clubs was not a member of the original Football League?
a) Manchester United
b) Aston Villa
c) Everton

10 Who was the 1992 Manager of the Year?
a) Kenny Dalglish
b) George Graham
c) Howard Wilkinson

Answers: 1.a 2.b 3.a 4.b 5.c 6.a 7.a 8.c 9.a 10.c

Monday May 31 1999

Tuesday June 1 1999

Wednesday June 2 1999

Thursday June 3 1999

Friday June 4 1999

Saturday June 5 1999

Sunday June 6 1999

Monday June 7 1999

Tuesday June 8 1999

Wednesday June 9 1999

Thursday June 10 1999

Friday June 11 1999

Saturday June 12 1999

Sunday June 13 1999

On 5 April, Newcastle United put their torrid season to one side to reach their first FA Cup Final for 24 years. A second-half strike by Alan Shearer, who was three years old last time the Magpies played in a Wembley final, settled the issue. The England striker's downward header was saved by Alan Kelly, but Shearer followed it up to strike home. Newcastle largely dominated proceedings but had keeper Shay Given to thank for two excellent late saves to ensure their progression. 'They've got quality players and after the first half, when they hit the post and had a couple kicked off the line, I knew it would be hard,' said Blades boss Steve Thompson.

ALLSPORT

Gary Speed aims to take Newcastle to Wembley, the first time in 24 years

'We did not deserve anything here. Barnsley showed a lot more spirit than us.' That was Ron Atkinson's verdict after his Sheffield Wednesday side slumped to a derby defeat against Tyke rivals Barnsley on 11 April. And it was a loss which edged the Owls ever closer to the drop-zone, just weeks after they looked safe for a mid-table berth. Ashley Ward opened the scoring, poking home from close range in the second half. Substitute Jan Fjortoft struck seven minutes later to guarantee Barnsley the three points, giving them a faint chance of beating the drop.

Even Guy Whittingham couldn't stop Barnsley rolling their neighbours in their encounter

ALLSPORT

Monday June 14 1999

Tuesday June 15 1999

Wednesday June 16 1999

Thursday June 17 1999

Friday June 18 1999

Saturday June 19 1999

Sunday June 20 1999

Monday June 21 1999

Tuesday June 22 1999

Wednesday June 23 1999

Thursday June 24 1999

Friday June 25 1999

Saturday June 26 1999

Sunday June 27 1999

25 April: Tottenham Hotspur won the crucial battle against relegation rivals Newcastle, with goals from frontmen Jürgen Klinsmann and Les Ferdinand. But the best performance of the day came from Spurs' midfielder David Ginola, who ran the Newcastle defence ragged all afternoon. The former Newcastle winger set up the first, when he turned neatly past Warren Barton on the right and his curling cross was met by the head of Klinsmann. And in the second half, Les Ferdinand nodded home a Ginola corner to give Spurs three vital points. Christian Gross was delighted with Ferdinand's return after injury: 'This was his best performance for me. He wants to save Spurs and go to the World Cup,' said Gross.

ALLSPORT

Running Newcastle ragged – the Klinsmann (& Ferdinand) show

Brave Barnsley's year in the Premiership ended in relegation at Leicester City on 2 May. The Tykes produced yet another battling performance at Filbert Street but fell to a second half goal from Theo Zagorakis, which proved enough to give Martin O'Neill's men an outside chance of European qualification. Barnsley did create opportunities but both Ashley Ward and Jan Aage Fjortoft were denied by Kasey Keller in the Leicester goal. Despite relegation, Tykes' boss Danny Wilson remained relatively upbeat. 'It was not just today's game but our performances throughout the season which have caused us to be relegated,' he said. But he add: 'In the second half of the season my players have been a credit to themselves – and me.'

ALLSPORT

Premiership survival or European glory?
Barnsley and Leicester battle for two prizes

1999 JUNE 28 – JULY 4

Monday June 28 1999

Tuesday June 29 1999

Wednesday June 30 1999

Thursday July 1 1999

Friday July 2 1999

Saturday July 3 1999

Sunday July 4 1999

ALLSPORT

Phew! A bit close, but at least there's another year for Everton to pull back from the brink

Arsenal were crowned champions for the first time since 1991, sealing the Premiership title with a 4–0 win over Everton at Highbury on 3 May. The Gunners got off to a great start when Emmanuel Petit's free kick was headed into his own net by Everton defender Slaven Bilic after just six minutes. Dutch winger Marc Overmars netted a brace to make the game safe before Tony Adams ran onto Steve Bould's through ball to finish superbly in the 89th minute. Arsene Wenger, the first foreign coach to a lead a side to the championship, was delighted. 'I always thought we could do it and everybody here has contributed to our success. We played like champions,' said Wenger. Arsenal skipper Tony Adams was delighted, too. 'I am determined to savour every moment. I don't remember too much from last time but I will this time.' he said.

Bolton Wanderers' brave fight for Premiership survival ended in failure at Stamford Bridge on 10 May. Colin Todd's men slipped through the trap door after a 2–0 defeat by Chelsea, but it was a cruel way to go down. Rivals Everton only survived because they conceded five fewer goals than Wanderers. Per Frandson had a first-half effort cleared off the line by Dennis Wise before Blues' player-boss Gianluca Vialli scored 15 minutes from time. And Jody Morris added a second near the death to send Bolton crashing. 'We came close to a great escape but I just couldn't manage it,' said a heartbroken Colin Todd afterwards. 'I feel sorry for the players and for our supporters.'

Everton survived relegation by the skin of their teeth, but after Dion Dublin equalised Gareth Farrelly's opener, the Goodison Park faithful had to endure a nail-biting finish. As it was, Farrelly's early strike – his first league goal since a summer switch from Aston Villa – has ensured Everton's start in the top league in the 199899 campaign, their 45th consecutive season. Nick Barmby should have made Everton safe in the 84th minute when Danny Cadamarteri was upended by Paul Williams, but the former Spurs striker's spot kick was saved by Hedman. Howard Kendall was a relieved man: 'This was a day I would not want to go through again and we won't as long as I am manager,' he said. Hmmm...

And that was 1997-98. Tony Adams and Arsene Wenger were ready for the FA Cup too

ALLSPORT

1998/99 PROGRESS CHART FOR SUPPORTERS OF

		DATE	SCORE	POINTS	PLACE	REFEREE
Chelsea ....v.................. Arsenal	HOME	/ /	–			
	AWAY	/ /	–			
Chelsea ....v.............. Aston Villa	HOME	/ /	–			
	AWAY	/ /	–			
Chelsea ....v .... Blackburn Rovers	HOME	/ /	–			
	AWAY	/ /	–			
Chelsea ....v......... Charlton Athletic	HOME	/ /	–			
	AWAY	/ /	–			
Chelsea ....v............ Coventry City	HOME	/ /	–			
	AWAY	/ /	–			
Chelsea ....v............ Derby County	HOME	/ /	–			
	AWAY	/ /	–			
Chelsea ....v................. Everton	HOME	/ /	–			
	AWAY	/ /	–			
Chelsea ....v .... Leeds United	HOME	/ /	–			
	AWAY	/ /	–			
Chelsea ....v............ Leicester City	HOME	/ /	–			
	AWAY	/ /	–			
Chelsea ....v................ Liverpool	HOME	/ /	–			
	AWAY	/ /	–			
Chelsea ....v....... Manchester United	HOME	/ /	–			
	AWAY	/ /	–			
Chelsea ....v .... Middlesbrough	HOME	/ /	–			
	AWAY	/ /	–			
Chelsea ....v .... Newcastle United	HOME	/ /	–			
	AWAY	/ /	–			
Chelsea ....v .... Nottingham Forest	HOME	/ /	–			
	AWAY	/ /	–			
Chelsea ....v ..... Sheffield Wednesday	HOME	/ /	–			
	AWAY	/ /	–			
Chelsea ....v............ Southampton	HOME	/ /	–			
	AWAY	/ /	–			
Chelsea ....v....... Tottenham Hotspur	HOME	/ /	–			
	AWAY	/ /	–			
Chelsea ....v......... West Ham United	HOME	/ /	–			
	AWAY	/ /	–			
Chelsea ....v.............. Wimbledon	HOME	/ /	–			
	AWAY	/ /	–			

MATCH NOTES

....

....

....

....

....

....

	GOALSCORERS	YELLOW CARDS	RED CARDS	COMMENTS

MATCH NOTES

SUPPORTERS' AWAY INFORMATION

UNITED KINGDOM AIRPORTS

Aberdeen (Dyce)	01224 722331
Belfast (Aldegrove)	01849 422888
Birmingham International	0121 767-5511
Blackpool	01253 343434
Bournemouth (Hurn)	01202 593939
Bristol (Luisgate)	01275 474444
Cambridge	01223 61133
Cardiff	01446 711211
East Midlands	01332 852852
Edinburgh	0131333-1000
Glasgow	0141 887 1111
Humberside	01652 688491
Inverness (Dalcross)	01463 232471
Leeds & Bradford (Yeadon)	01132 509696
Liverpool (Speke)	0151 486-8877
London (Gatwick)	01293 535353
London (Heathrow)	0181 759-4321
London (London City)	0171 474-5555
London (Stanstead)	01279 680500
Luton	01582 405100
Lydd	01797 320401
Manchester (Ringway)	0161 489-3000
Newcastle (Woolsington)	0191 286-0966
Newquay (St. Mawgan)	01637 860551
Norwich	01603 411923
Plymouth	01752 772752
Prestwick	01292 479822
Southampton	01703 629600
Southend	01702 340201
Stornoway	01851 702256
Teesside (Darlington)	01325 332811
Westland Heliport	0171 228-0181

PASSPORT OFFICES

London 0171 799-2728
Clive House, 70–78 Petty France, SW1H 9HD

Liverpool 0151 237-3010
5th Floor, India Buildings, Water Street, L2 0QZ

Peterborough 01733 555688
UK Passport Agency, Aragon Court, Northminster Road, Peterborough PE1 1QG

Glasgow 0141 332-4441
3 Northgate, 96 Milton Street, Cowcadens, Glasgow G4 0BT

Newport 01633 473700
Olympia House, Upper Dock Street, Newport, Gwent NP9 1XQ

Belfast 01232 330214
Hampton House, 47–53 High Street, Belfast BT1 2QS

TOURIST & TRAVEL INFORMATION CENTRES

ENGLAND

Birmingham (NEC)	0121 780-4321
Blackpool	01253 21623
Bournemouth	01202 789789
Brighton	01273 323755
Cambridge	01223 322640
Chester	01244 351609
Colchester	01206 282920
Dover	01304 205108
Durham	0191 384-3720
Hull	01482 223559
Lancaster	01524 32878
Leicester	01162 650555
Lincoln	01522 529828
Liverpool	0151 708-8838
Manchester	0161 234-3157
Newcastle-upon-Tyne	0191 261-0691
Newquay	01603 871345
Norwich	01603 666071
Oxford	01865 726871
Portsmouth	01705 826722
Southampton	01703 221106
Torquay	01803 297428
York	01904 620557

SCOTLAND

Aberdeen	01224 632727
Edinburgh	0131 557-1700
Glasgow	0141 848-4440
Stirling	01786 475019

WALES

Cardiff	01222 227281
Wrexham	01978 292015

MAIN INTER-CITY RAIL CONNECTIONS FOR SCOTLAND

MAIN INTER-CITY RAIL CONNECTIONS FOR

ENGLAND & WALES

FERRY SERVICES

B&I Line	Liverpool	0151 2273131
Brittany Ferries	Plymouth	01752 221321
Color Line	Newcastle	0191 2961313
Hoverspeed	Dover	01304 240241
North Sea Ferries	Hull	01482 795141
Olau Line	Sheerness	01795 666666
P&O European	Dover	01304 203388
P&O Scottish	Aberdeen	01224 589111
Scandinavian	Harwich	01255 240240
Stena Sealink	Ashford	01233 647047
Swansea Cork	Swansea	01792 456116

TRAIN OPERATOR CONTACTS

See following page

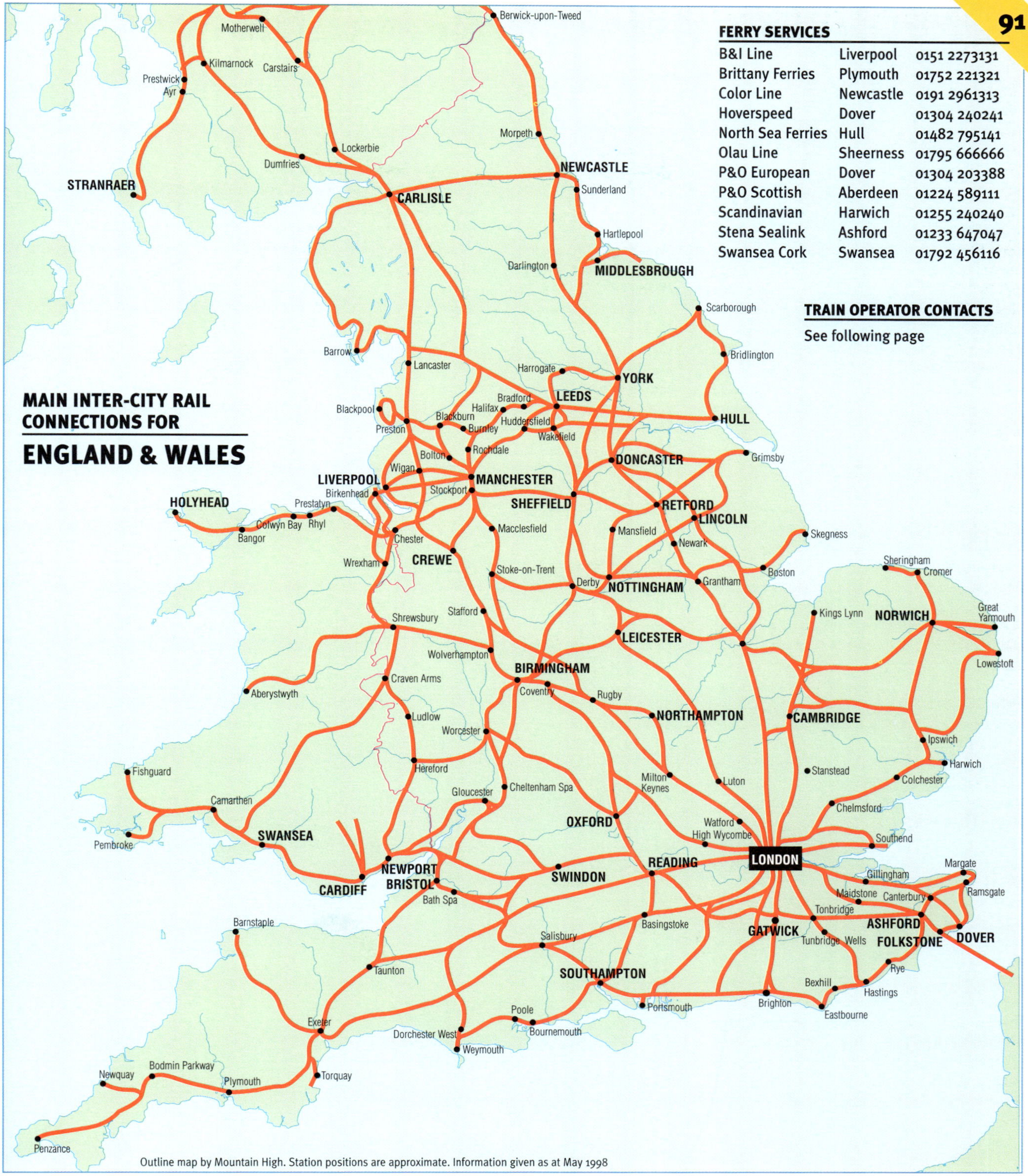

Outline map by Mountain High. Station positions are approximate. Information given as at May 1998

SUPPORTERS' AWAY INFORMATION

TRAIN OPERATORS

ANGLIA RAILWAYS
15-25 Artillery Lane, London, E1 7HA
Tel 01473 693333
Fax 01473 693497

CARDIFF RAILWAY CO
10th Floor, Brunel House, 2 Fitzalan Rd,
Cardiff CF2 1SA
Tel 01222 430000
Fax 01222 480463

CENTRAL TRAINS
PO Box 4323, Stanier House, 10 Holliday Street
Birmingham B1 1TH
Tel 0121 654 4444
Fax 0121 654 4461

CHILTERN RAILWAY CO
Western House, 14 Rickfords Hill, Aylesbury
HP20 2RX
Tel 01296 332100
Fax 01296 332126

CONNEX SOUTH CENTRAL
Stephenson House, 2 Cherry Orchard Road,
Croydon CR9 6JB
Tel 0181 667 2780
Fax 0181 667 2906

EUROSTAR (UK)
Eurostar House, Waterloo Station, London
SE1 8SE
Tel 0171 928 5151

GATWICK EXPRESS
52 Grosvenor Gardens, London SW1W OAU
Tel 0171 973 5005
Fax 0171 973 5038

GREAT EASTERN RAILWAY
Hamilton House, 3 Appold Street, London
EC2A 2AA
Tel 0645 50 50 00
Fax 01473 693745

GREAT NORTH EATERN RAILWAY
Main Headquarters Building, York YO1 1HT
Tel 01904 653022
Fax 01904 523392

GREAT WESTERN TRAINS CO
Milford House, 1 Milton Street, Swindon SN1 1HL
Tel 01793 499400
Fax 01793 499460

HEATHROW EXPRESS
4th Floor, Cardinal Point, Newall Rd, Hounslow
Middlesex TW6 2QS
Tel 0181 745 0578
Fax 0181 745 1627

ISLAND LINE
Ryde St Johns Road Station, Ryde, Isle Of Wight
PO33 2BA
Tel 01983 812591
Fax 01983 817879

LTS RAIL
Central House, Clifftown Road, Southend-on-Sea
SS1 1AB
Tel 01702 357889

MERSEYRAIL ELECTRICS
Rail House, Lord Nelson Street, Liverpool L1 1JF
Tel 0151 709 8292
Fax 0151 702 2413

MIDLAND MAINLINE
Midland House, Nelson Street, Derby,
East Midlands DE1 2SA
Tel 0345 221125
Fax 01332 262011

NORTH WESTERN TRAINS
PO Box 44, Rail House, Store Street
Manchester M60 1DQ
Tel 0161 228 2141
Fax 0161 228 5003

REGIONAL RAILWAYS NORTH EAST
Main Headquarters Building, York YO1 1HT
Tel 01904 653022

SCOTRAIL RAILWAYS
Caledonian Chambers, 87 Union Street
Glasgow G1 3TA
Tel 0141 332 9811

SILVERLINK TRAIN SERVICES
65-67 Clarendon Raod, Watford WD1 1DP
Tel 01923 207258
Fax 01923 207023

SOUTH WEST TRAINS
Friars Bridge Court, 41-45 Blackfrairs Road
London SE1 8NZ
Tel 0171 928 5151
Fax 0171 902 3208

THAMESLINK RAIL
Friars Bridge, 41-45 Blackfriars Road,
London SE1 8NZ
Tel 0171 620 5760
Fax 0171 620 5099

THAMES TRAINS
Venture House, 37 Blagrave Street, Reading
RG1 1PZ
Tel 0118 908 3678
Fax 0118 957 9006

VIRGIN TRAINS
85 Smallbrook Queensway, Birmingham B5 4HA
Tel 0121 654 7400
Fax 0121 654 7487

WALES & WEST
Brunel House, 2 Fitzalan Rd, Cardiff CF2 1SU
Tel 01222 430400
Fax 01222 430214

WEST ANGLIA GREAT NORTHERN RAILWAY
Hertford House, 1 Cranwood Street, London
EC1V 9GT
Tel 0345 818919
Fax 01223 453606

WEST COAST RAILWAY COMPANY
Warton Road, Carnforth, Lancashire LA5 9HX
Tel 01524 732100
Fax 01524 735518

SOCCER RELATED INTERNET BOOKMARKS

The following three pages are a listing of soccer websites, some of which you may find useful to bookmark. As any internet browser will know all too well, URLs change, move or become obsolete at the drop of a hat. At the time of going to press all the ones listed were active.

If you are new to internet browsing, the following information on entering the URL addresses should be observed. Because of the way the address lines are printed, those longer than the width of the column are broken into two lines, the second slightly indented. Nevertheless, all the characters of the address should be typed in as one line, with no spaces between characters. If your edition or version of browser already enters the 'http://' characters, or does not require them, omit these from the URL address.

Where sites are official, it states so in brackets after the site name. Any useful notes about the site are given after the name in square brackets.

WORLD CUP RELATED PAGES

Football Web in Japan
http://www.nidnet.com/link/socweb.html
CBS SportsLine - Soccer
http://www.sportsline.com/u/soccer/index.html
Teams of the World
http://www.islandia.is/totw/
World Cup - Soccernet
http://www.soccernet.com/u/soccer/worldcup98/index.html
World Cup 1998 - CBS SportsLine
http://www.sportsline.com/u/soccer/worldcup98/qualifying/index.html
World Cup Soccer - France 98 - Coupe du Monde
http://www.worldcup.com/english/index.html

FOOTBALL RELATED

1997 edition of the Laws of the Game
http://www.fifa.com/fifa/handbook/laws/index.laws.html
Soccer Books [good reference]
http://www.soccer-books.co.uk
British Society of Sports History [reference material]
http://www.umist.ac.uk/UMIST_Sport/bssh.html
Buchanan Brigade Messge Bd Thirty-Three
http://www.buchanan.org/mb33.html
Communicata Football
http://www.communicata.co.uk/lookover/football/
Division 1 Web Pages [relates to the Nationwide leagues]
http://www.users.globalnet.co.uk/~emmas/ndiv1.htm
Division 2 Web Pages [old Endsleigh rather than the Nationwide]
http://www.uwm.edu/People/dyce/htfc/clubs/div2-www.html
England [Engerland]
http://www.users.dircon.co.uk/~england/england/
England [Green Flags England team pages]
http://www.greenflag.co.uk/te/fslist.html
England [English Soccernet - National Team - News]
http://www.soccernet.com/english/national/news/index.html
England
http://www.englandfc.com/
English Club Homepages
http://pluto.webbernet.net/~bob/engclub.html
FAI - Irish International
http://www.fai.ie/
GeordieSport!
http://www.geordiepride.demon.co.uk/geordiesport.htm
L & M Referees' Society - Soccer Pages
http://www.lancs.ac.uk/ug/williams/soccer.htm
Northern Ireland [Norn Iron!: The NI International Football 'zine]
http://students.un.umist.ac.uk/gbh/index.html
Notts Association
http://www.innotts.co.uk/~soccerstats/gallery/nmf8.htm
Scotland [Rampant Scotland - Sport]
http://scotland.rampant.com/sport.htm
Scotland
http://web.city.ac.uk/~sh393/euro/scotland.htm
Scottish Football Association (Official)
http://www.scottishfa.co.uk/
Scottish Mailing Lists
http://www.isfa.com/isfa/lists/scotland.htm
Simply the Best
http://www.int-foot-fame.com/famers1.htm
Soccer ScoreSheet History List
http://www.kazmax.demon.co.uk/websheet/tm000309.htm
Soccer-Tables
http://www.marwin.ch/sport/fb/index.e.html
SoccerSearch: Players:G-P
http://www.soccersearch.com/Players/G-P/
SoccerSpace, Football & Soccer Links
http://www.winbet.sci.fi/soccerspace/links.htm
Team England - Fixtures & Results
http://ourworld.compuserve.com/homepages/nic_king/england/fixtures.htm
The Association of Football Statisticians
http://www.innotts.co.uk/~soccerstats/
The Aylesbury Branch of the Referees Association
http://homepages.bucks.net/~bigmick/
The Daily Soccer
http://www.dailysoccer.com/
The Football Supporters' Association (FSA)
http://www.fsa.org.uk/
US Soccer History Archives
http://www.sover.net/~spectrum/index.html
Welsh Football,Football wales,faw,welsh fa,ryan giggs
http://www.citypages.co.uk/faw/

ENGLISH PREMIERSHIP

Arsenal
http://www.arsenal.co.uk/
Aston Villa
http://www.geocities.com/Colosseum/Field/6089/
Aston Villa
http://www.villan.demon.co.uk/
Aston Villa
http://www.gbar.dtu.dk/~c937079/AVFC/index.html
Aston Villa (Official)
http://www.gbar.dtu.dk/~c937079/CB/
Barnsley
http://www.geocities.com/Colosseum/Field/6059/bfc.html
Barnsley
http://www.u-net.com/westex/bfc.htm
Barnsley
http://www.radders.skynet.co.uk/
Barnsley
http://upload.virgin.net/d.penty/Copacabarnsley/Copacabarnsley.htm
Barnsley
http://members.aol.com/JLister/bfc/bfc.htm
Blackburn Rovers
http://www.brfc-supporters.org.uk/
Blackburn Rovers (Official)
http://www.rovers.co.uk/
Bolton Wanderers
http://www.hankins.demon.co.uk/bwscl/index.html
Bolton Wanderers
http://www.netcomuk.co.uk/~cjw/football.html
Bolton Wanderers
http://www.geocities.com/Colosseum/4433/
Bolton Wanderers
http://mail.freeway.co.uk/druid/
Bolton Wanderers (Official)
http://www.boltonwfc.co.uk/
Charlton Athletic
http://www.demon.co.uk/casc/index.html
Chelsea
http://www.geocities.com/Colosseum/1457/chelsea.html
Chelsea
http://web.ukonline.co.uk/Members/jf.lettice/cfcmain.html
Chelsea
http://www.jack.dircon.net/chelsea/
Chelsea
http://fans-of.chelsea-fc.com/csr/
Chelsea FC (Official)
http://www.chelseafc.co.uk/chelsea/frontpage.shtml
Coventry City [mpegs of goals... that's it]
http://karpaty.tor.soliton.com/ccfcgoals/
Coventry City [The Sky Blue Superplex]
http://www.geocities.com/TimesSquare/Dungeon/1641/page4.html
Coventry City
http://www.warwick.ac.uk/~cudbu/SkyBlues.html
Coventry City (Official)
http://www.ccfc.co.uk/
Derby County
http://lard.sel.cam.ac.uk/derby_county/
Derby County
http://www.cheme.cornell.edu/~jwillits/this.html
Derby County
http://easyweb.easynet.co.uk/~nickwheat/ramsnet.html
Derby County
http://home.sol.no/~einasand/derby.htm
Derby County
http://www.cheme.cornell.edu/~jwillits/derby2.html#History
Derby County
http://www.derby-county.com/main.htm
Derby County (Official)
http://www.dcfc.co.uk/dcfc/index.html
Everton FC (Official)
http://www.connect.org.uk/everton/
Leeds United
http://www.lufc.co.uk/
Leeds United
http://spectrum.tcns.co.uk/cedar/leeds.htm
Leeds United
http://www.csc.liv.ac.uk/users/tim/Leeds/
Leeds United (Official - CarlingNet)
http://www.fa-premier.com/club/lufc/
Leicester City (Official)
http://www.lcfc.co.uk/141097b.htm
Liverpool
http://akureyri.ismennt.is/~jongeir/
Liverpool
http://www.soccernet.com/livrpool/
Liverpool
http://www.connect.org.uk/anfield/
Manchester United
http://www.cs.indiana.edu/hyplan/ccheah/posts.html
Manchester United
http://www.geocities.com/SouthBeach/6367/index.html
Manchester United
http://www.sky.co.uk/sports/manu/
Manchester United
http://www.cybernet.dk/users/barrystorv/
Manchester United
http://home.pacific.net.sg/~jerping/
Manchester United
http://sunhehi.phy.uic.edu/~clive/MUFC/home.html
Manchester United
http://www.iol.ie/~mmurphy/red_devils/mufc.htm
Manchester United
http://www.davewest.demon.co.uk/
Manchester United
http://www.webcom.com/~solution/mufc/manu.html
Manchester United
http://ourworld.compuserve.com/homepages/red_devil/
Manchester United
http://xanadu.centrum.is/~runarhi/
Manchester United
http://web.city.ac.uk/~sh393/mufc.htm
Manchester United
http://www.wsu.edu:8080/~mmarks/Giggs.html
Manchester United
http://osiris.sunderland.ac.uk/online/access/manutd/redshome.html
Manchester United
http://www.u-net.com/~pitman/
Manchester United
http://www.geocities.com/Colosseum/2483/
Manchester United
http://www.wsu.edu:8080/~mmarks/mufclinks.html
Manchester United
http://gladstone.uoregon.edu:80/~jsetzen/mufc.html
Manchester United
http://members.hknet.com/~siukin/
Newcastle United
http://www.swan.co.uk/TOTT
Newcastle United
http://www.nufc.com
Newcastle United
http://www.btinternet.com/~the.magpie/history1.htm
Newcastle United
http://www.ccacyber.com/nufc/
Newcastle United
http://sunflower.singnet.com.sg/~resa21/
Nottingham Forest
http://users.homenet.ie/~aidanhut/
Nottingham Forest
http://www.thrustworld.co.uk/users/kryten/forest/
Nottingham Forest
http://hem1.passagen.se/pearce/index.htm
Nottingham Forest
http://www.innotts.co.uk/~joe90/forest.htm
Nottingham Forest
http://ourworld.compuserve.com/homepages/kencrossland/
Nottingham Forest (Official)
http://www.nottingham-forest.co.uk/frames.html
Sheffield Wednesday
http://www.crg.cs.nott.ac.uk/Users/anb/Football/stats/swfcarch.htm
Sheffield Wednesday
http://www.rhi.hi.is/~jbj/sheffwed/opnun.htm

BOOKMARKS

Sheffield Wednesday
http://www.geocities.com/Colosseum/2938/
Sheffield Wednesday
http://www.cs.nott.ac.uk/~anb/Football/
Southampton [Saintsweb]
http://www.soton.ac.uk/~saints/
Southampton [Marching In]
http://www.saintsfans.com/marchingin/
Tottenham Hotspur [White Hart Site]
http://www.xpress.se/~ssab0019/webring/index.html
Tottenham Hotspur [Felix Gills' Page]
http://www.gilnet.demon.co.uk/spurs.htm
Tottenham Hotspur
http://www.personal.u-net.com/~spurs/
Tottenham Hotspur [check Spurs results year-by-year - just stats]
http://www.bobexcell.demon.co.uk/
Tottenham Hotspur
http://www.btinternet.com/~matt.cook/
Tottenham Hotspur (Official)
http://www.spurs.co.uk/welcome.html
West Ham United
http://www.ecs.soton.ac.uk/saints/premier/westham.htm
West Ham United
http://www.westhamunited.co.uk/
Wimbledon
http://www.fa-premier.com/cgi-bin/fetch/club/wfc/home.html?team='WIM'
Wimbledon [unofficial - WISA]
http://www.wisa.org.uk/
Wimbledon [Womble.Net - Independent Wimbledon FC Internet 'zine]
http://www.geocities.com/SunsetStrip/Studio/6112/womblnet.html
Wimbledon [very basic]
http://www.aracnet.com/~davej/football.htm
Wimbledon [unofficial - USA]
http://soyokaze.biosci.ohio-state.edu/~dcp/wimbledon/womble.html
Wimbledon
http://www.city.ac.uk/~sh393/prem/wimbeldon.htm
Wimbledon
http://www.netkonect.co.uk/b/brenford/wimbledon/
Wimbledon [unofficial - WISA]
http://www.soi.city.ac.uk/homes/ec564/donswisa.html
Wimbledon [John's Wimbledon FC page]
http://www.soi.city.ac.uk/homes/ec564/dons.top.html
Wimbledon (Official)
http://www.wimbledon-fc.co.uk/

ENGLISH DIVISION 1

Birmingham City [PlanetBlues]
http://www.isfa.com/server/web/planetblues/
Birmingham City [BCFC Supports Club Redditch Branch]
http://www.fortunecity.com/olympia/ovett/135/
Birmingham City [Richy's B'ham City Page]
http://www.rshill.demon.co.uk/blues.htm
Bradford City
http://www.legend.co.uk/citygent/index.html
Bury
http://www.brad.ac.uk/%7edjmartin/bury1.html
Crystal Palace
http://www.gold.net/users/az21/cp_home.htm
Fulham [The Independent Fulham Fans Website: History]
http://www.fulhamfc.co.uk/History/history.html
Fulham [FulhamWeb]
http://www.btinternet.com/~aredfern/
Fulham [Black & White Pages]
http://www.wilf.demon.co.uk/fulhamfc/ffc.html
Fulham [unofficial - The Fulham Football Club Mailing List]
http://www.users.dircon.co.uk/~troyj/fulham/
Fulham
http://zeus.bris.ac.uk/~chmsl/fulham/fulham.html
Fulham
http://www.netlondon.com/cgi-local/wilma/spo.873399737.html
Fulham (Official) [mostly merchandising]
http://www.fulham-fc.co.uk/
Huddersfield Town
http://www.geocities.com/Colosseum/4401/index.html
Huddersfield Town
http://ftp.csd.uwm.edu/People/dyce/htfc/
Huddersfield Town
http://granby.nott.ac.uk/~ppykara/htfc/
Huddersfield Town
http://www.uwm.edu:80/~dyce/htfc/index.html
Ipswich Town [MATCHfacts - Datafile]
http://www.matchfacts.com/mfdclub/ipswich.htm
Ipswich Town
http://www.sys.uea.ac.uk/Recreation/Sport/itfc/
Ipswich Town [Those Were The Days]
http://www.twtd.co.uk/
Ipswich Town
http://members.wbs.net/homepages/a/d/a/adamcable.html
Ipswich Town [The Online Portman Vista]
http://www.btinternet.com/~bluearmy/index2.html
Ipswich Town [unofficial - Latest News - not really]
http://www.rangey.demon.co.uk/ipswich.htm
Ipswich Town [IPSWICH TOWN tribute]
http://www.geocities.com/Colosseum/Track/5399/
Ipswich Town [The Ipswich Town VRML Site - techy, not much else]
http://www.sys.uea.ac.uk/Recreation/Sport/itfc/vrml/vrml.html
Ipswich Town
http://homepages.enterprise.net/meo/itfc2.html
Ipswich Town (Official)
http://www.itfc.co.uk/
Manchester City
http://www.uit.no/mancity/
Manchester City (Official)
http://www.mcfc.co.uk/
Middlesbrough
http://www.hk.super.net/~tlloyd/personal/boro.html
Norwich City
http://ncfc.netcom.co.uk/ncfc/
Oxford United
http://www.aligrafix.co.uk/ag/fun/home/OxTales/default.html
Oxford United
http://www.netlink.co.uk//users/oufc1/index.html
Port Vale
http://www.netcentral.co.uk/~iglover/index.html
Port Vale
http://web.dcs.hull.ac.uk/people/pjp/PortVale/PortVale.html
Portsmouth [unofficial - History]
http://www.mech.port.ac.uk/StaffP/pb/history.html
Portsmouth [Links page]
http://www.imsport.co.uk/imsport/ims/tt/035/club.html
Queens Park Rangers
http://www-dept.cs.ucl.ac.uk/students/M.Pemble/index.html
Reading
http://www.i-way.co.uk/~readingfc/
Sheffield United
http://www.shef.ac.uk/city/blades/
Sheffield United
http://pine.shu.ac.uk/~cmssa/bifa.html
Sheffield United (Official)
http://www.sufc.co.uk/
Stoke City
http://www.cs.bham.ac.uk/~jdr/scfc/scfc.htm
Sunderland (Official)
http://www.sunderland-afc.com/
Swindon Town
http://www.bath.ac.uk/~ee3cmk/swindon/home.html
Tranmere Rovers
http://www.connect.org.uk/merseyworld/tarantula/
Tranmere Rovers
http://www.brad.ac.uk/~mjhesp/tran.htm
West Bromwich Albion
http://pages.prodigy.com/FL/baggie/
West Bromwich Albion
http://www.gold.net/users/cp78/
West Bromwich Albion - Official
http://www.wba.co.uk/
Wolverhampton Wanderers [The Wandering Wolf]
http://www.angelfire.com/wv/Quants/index.html
Wolverhampton Wanderers
http://www.lazy-dog.demon.co.uk/wolves/
Wolverhampton Wanderers (Official)
http://www.idiscover.co.uk/wolves/

ENGLISH DIVISION 2

AFC Bournemouth
http://www.bath.ac.uk/~ee6dlah/club.htm
AFC Bournemouth
http://www.homeusers.prestel.co.uk/rose220/afcb1.htm
AFC Bournemouth
http://www.maths.soton.ac.uk/rpb/AFCB.html
AFC Bournemouth
http://www.maths.soton.ac.uk/rpb/AFCB.html
AFC Bournemouth
http://www.geocities.com/TimesSquare/Arcade/7499/afcb.htm
AFC Bournemouth (Official)
http://www.afcb.co.uk/
Blackpool
http://web.ukonline.co.uk/Members/c.moffat/basil/
Bristol City
http://ourworld.compuserve.com/homepages/redrobins/
Bristol Rovers
http://dialspace.dial.pipex.com/town/street/xko88/
Bristol Rovers
http://members.wbs.net/homepages/l/a/r/lardon/
Bristol Rovers
http://www.cf.ac.uk/uwcc/engin/brittonr/rovers/index.html
Bristol Rovers
http://www.geocities.com/Colosseum/6542/
Bristol Rovers
http://www.personal.unet.com/~coley/rovers/
Bristol Rovers
http://www.btinternet.com/~uk/BRFC/
Bristol Rovers
http://www.btinternet.com/~uk/BristolRovers/index.html
Bristol Rovers
http://www.cowan.edu.au/~gprewett/gas.htm
Bristol Rovers
http://www.cf.ac.uk/uwcc/engin/brittonr/rovers/index.html
Burnley
http://www.zensys.co.uk/home/page/trevor.ent/
Burnley
http://www.theturf.demon.co.uk/burnley.htm
Burnley
http://www.zen.co.uk/home/page/p.bassek/
Burnley
http://www.mtattersall.demon.co.uk/index.html
Burnley
http://home.sol.no/~parald/burnley/
Burnley
http://www.geocities.com/Colosseum/7075/index.html
Carlisle United
http://www.aston.ac.uk/~jonespm/
Carlisle United
http://dspace.dial.pipex.com/town/square/ad969/
Chester City [Silly Sausage - good history]
http://www.sillysausage.demon.co.uk/history.htm
Chester City (Official)
http://www.chester-city.co.uk/
Gillingham
http://ourworld.compuserve.com/homepages/gillsf.c/
Grimsby Town
http://www.aston.ac.uk/~etherina/index.html
Preston North End [unofficial - PNEWeb HomePage]
http://freespace.virgin.net/paul.billington/PNEWeb_homepage.html
Preston North End [unofficial - PNE Pages]
http://www.dpne.demon.co.uk/pages/pagesf.html
Preston North End [pie muncher online - front door]
http://www.pylonvu.demon.co.uk/pm/pm.html

Swansea City
http://www2.prestel.co.uk/gmartin/index.html
Wrexham
http://www.aber.ac.uk/~deg/wxm/text.html
Wrexham
http://www.csm.uwe.ac.uk/~klhender/wxm/index.html
Wycombe Wanderers
http://ourworld.compuserve.com/homepages/chairboys/

ENGLISH DIVISION 3

Brighton and Hove Albion
http://www.bmharding.demon.co.uk/seagulls/index.html/
Brighton and Hove Albion
http://homepages.enterprise.net/gjc/
Brighton and Hove Albion
http://www.aber.ac.uk/~bmh1/seagulls/
Cardiff City (Official)
http://www.styrotech.co.uk/ccafc/
Cardiff City
http://www.cf.ac.uk/uwcm/mg/bloo/biz.html
Cardiff City
http://www.geocities.com/Colosseum/1943/
Cardiff City
http://ds.dial.pipex.com/m4morris/ccafc.htm
Chester City
http://www.sillysausage.demon.co.uk/others.htm
Halifax Town
http://www.geocities.com/Colosseum/Stadium/3043/
Halifax Town [Aussie Style]
http://expage.com/page/Shaymen
Halifax Town [Shaymen]
http://www.shaymen.clara.net/shaymen.html
Hull City
http://www.demon.co.uk/Vox/hullcity/hullcity.html
Hull City
http://www.hullcity.demon.co.uk/
Leyton Orient (Official -OriNet)
http://www.matchroom.com/orient/
Leyton Orient [WebOrient - Global Orient Website]
http://www.web-orient.clara.net/
Macclesfield Town
http://www.cs.man.ac.uk/~griffitm/macctown/
Mansfield Town
http://www.footballnews.co.uk/clubs/1068/home.htm
Notts County
http://home.sol.no/~benn/magpienet/
Notts County
http://www.nbs.ntu.ac.uk/Staff/baylidj/ncfc.htm
Notts County
http://www.nbs.ntu.ac.uk/Staff/baylidj/ncfc.htm
Notts County
http://www.athene.net/soccercity/europe/eng/nc.htm
Notts County
http://www.imsport.co.uk/imsport/ims/tt/032/032.html
Scunthorpe United [The Iron Network]
http://www.fortunecity.com/wembley/villa/56/index.html
Scunthorpe United [Mailing List]
http://www.isfa.com/isfa/lists/scunthorpe/
Scunthorpe United [Iron World]
http://freespace.virgin.net/su.fc/
Shrewsbury Town
http://www.netlink.co.uk/users/ian/shrews/shrews.html
Shrewsbury Town
http://www.shrewsburytown.co.uk/
Swansea City
http://homepages.enterprise.net/gmartin/
Swansea City
http://homepages.enterprise.net/gmartin/indexnf.html

SCOTTISH PREMIER LEAGUE

Aberdeen - Official
http://www.afc.co.uk/site/
Aberdeen
http://homepages.enterprise.net/howburn/
Aberdeen
http://www.web13.co.uk/dons/
Aberdeen
http://www.raik.grid9.net/dons/
Aberdeen
http://www.raik.demon.co.uk/dons/
Aberdeen
http://freespace.virgin.net/a.morrison/ajm/afchome2.htm
Celtic (Official)
http://www.celticfc.co.uk/presecurity2.html
Celtic
http://www.erols.com/gbrown/dccelts.htm
Celtic
http://www.presence.co.uk/soccer/pages/history.html
Dundee United
http://www.algonet.se/~snoe/dfc/
Dundee United
http://www.arabland.demon.co.uk/news.htm
Dunfermline Athletic
http://www.webadvertising.co.uk/wwwboard/pars2/
Dunfermline Athletic [Soccernet]
http://www.soccernet.com/scottish/dafc/index.html
Dunfermline Athletic
http://www.aiai.ed.ac.uk/~wth/dunfermline/dunfermline.html
Heart of Midlothian (Official)
http://www.heartsfc.co.uk/
Heart of Midlothian [No Idle Talk - okay]
http://web.ukonline.co.uk/Members/grant.thorburn/nit1.htm
Heart of Midlothian
http://jambos.aurdev.com/update.html
Heart of Midlothian [has a squad list. USA]
http://www.geocities.com/Colosseum/Arena/2659/
Heart of Midlothian [Electronic Jam Tart]
http://www.ednet.co.uk/~ricw/
Heart of Midlothian [M'chester Hearts fans]
http://www.rigor.demon.co.uk/manheart.htm
Heart of Midlothian [OrwellHeartsSC]
http://members.aol.com/orwellhsc/orwellhearts/index.html
Heart of Midlothian [Midlands Hearts]
http://members.aol.com/gsha27/midlandhearts1.htm
Heart of Midlothian [Hearts Supporters USA - not very informative]
http://jambos.aurdev.com/
Heart of Midlothian [Always The Bridesmaid]
http://ourworld.compuserve.com/homepages/a_macdougall_and_ATB/
Heart of Midlothian [Rainbow Hearts S.C. Homepage]
http://ourworld.compuserve.com/homepages/andy_rainbow_hearts/
Kilmarnock
http://homepages.enterprise.net/wallace/
Kilmarnock
http://www.enterprise.net/kilmarnockfc/index.htm
Motherwell
http://www.isfa.com/server/web/motherwell/
Rangers (Official) [you need to register]
http://www.rangers.co.uk/channels/
Rangers
http://www.ukfootballpages.com/rangers/
Rangers
http://www.cee.hw.ac.uk/~johnc/Rangers/homepage.html
Rangers
http://www.geocities.com/Tokyo/Flats/5554/home.html
Rangers
http://www.geocities.com/Colosseum/Field/2968/
Rangers
http://dspace.dial.pipex.com/x-static/rangers.htm
Rangers
http://www.sgwoozy.force9.co.uk/rangers.html
Rangers
http://www.geocities.com/Colosseum/Track/7990/
Rangers
http://members.aol.com/broxinet/index.html

WEBSITE NOTES

WIN A FREE FOOTBALL BOOK!

Thank-you for buying a copy of our soccer yearbooks, covering all teams in the English Premiership, Scottish Premiership, and English Divisions 1, 2 and 3. We hope that you are happy with your purchase.

This unique collection of yearbooks, gives each supporter in the land their own club diary, supported by all-action shots from the greatest highlights of the last season, plus a diary from July 1998 – June 1999, detailing all club fixtures for the season.

If you would like to be kept informed of other football titles and next season's yearbooks, please cut out and complete this form and mail it back to me: Sharon Pitcher – Marketing Manager, Parragon, 13 Whiteladies Road, Bristol, BS8 1PB. Ten Lucky respondents will receive a free football book for their trouble!

Name of Favourite
Team(s) ....
....

Name of Local
Team(s) ....
....

Where did you
buy this book? ....

Your Name: ....

Street: ....

Town: ....

County: ....

Postcode: ....

Email: ....

❏ Yes – please keep me informed of other football titles, plus next season's football yearbooks.

This information is being collected on behalf of Parragon Book Services Ltd.

For office use only

THE FAMILY T
DETECTIVE BOOK

Margaret Crush

Colour illustrations by
John Hersey and Chris Wojcicki

YOUNG LIBRARY

The clue

The mysterious old cabinet was battered and scratched, and smelt very musty. Some of its handles were missing. Gingerly, Sophie pulled out one of the tiny drawers. It was empty. She pulled out another. Nothing there either. One by

Grandpa G's cabinet, where the photo and embroidered postcard were found.

one she peered in each drawer: all empty.

Her younger brother, Ben, was fiddling with a carved panel. Suddenly . . . click! The panel slid up and back.

'A secret drawer!' he shouted.

Sophie was thrilled. Cautiously she slid her hand into the space and felt carefully around. The space wasn't empty after all.

'There's something there!' she whispered.

Slowly, she pulled the 'something' out. It was a faded yellow envelope. Inside, wrapped in some crumpled tissue paper going brown at the edges, was a postcard. It wasn't an ordinary postcard.

A recent school photo of Ben Trevor.

An old school photo of Sophie Trevor.

Instead of a picture, there was an embroidered wreath of flowers entwined with two Union Flags. Underneath, in golden thread, were stitched the words: *To my Dear Girl*. And on the back of the postcard were some words in faint pencil: *With best love to Florence, from Hubert*.

Ben pushed his hand into the secret drawer. He too felt carefully around; then he pulled out a crumpled brown photograph. It showed a young man in soldier's uniform . . . .

The cabinet was in Sophie and Ben's grand-parents' house. Grandpa G was very intrigued by their finds. The cabinet had belonged to his mother, but she had never shown him the secret drawer.

'That's a First World War uniform,' he announced, studying the faded photograph. 'My father fought in that war, the 1914–18, but this isn't a picture of him.'

'How romantic!' sighed Grandma G. 'Perhaps the young man is the Hubert who sent your

mother this postcard. Her name *was* Florence.'

Ben found it a bit difficult to imagine people as old as his grandparents having mothers and fathers. He said so quietly to Sophie. But not quietly enough. Grandpa G heard him and laughed.

'Here,' he said, 'let me draw you a family tree. It's a special sort of chart to show how everybody in a family is related to each other. 'See,' he drew busily, 'it is roughly in the shape of a tree. You kids are the narrow trunk at the bottom. The branches are your parents, grandparents, and so on, right back to the first prehistoric people from whom everybody in the world today is descended.'

'Of course, nobody could trace their ancestors that far back!' said Grandma G. 'But you could probably trace back a hundred years or so fairly easily. The study of family history is fun. It's rather like a jigsaw puzzle – you gradually fit the pieces of information into place.'

'Or like being a detective,' continued Grandpa G. 'You start with a few clues and try to solve the whole mystery. That postcard is your first clue.'

'That's it!' shouted Sophie. 'We'll be the Family Tree Detectives.'

Grandpa G showed Sophie and Ben how to draw a family tree. Start at the base of the trunk with yourself. Then split the tree into two branches – your Mum and Dad; and from there into more branches for their parents (your grandparents); and so on.

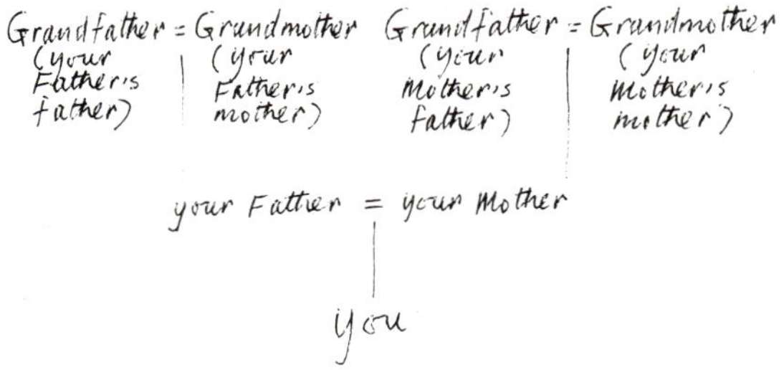

The search begins

Back home, Sophie and Ben found Uncle Roger (Dad's brother) drinking coffee in the kitchen and chatting to their mother. Excitedly, Sophie described their find.

'We're going to do our family tree!' announced Ben.

'We know Grandpa G's mother's name,' added Sophie. 'It was Florence. We're going to find out her parents' names and put another branch on the tree.'

'Wait a minute,' laughed Uncle Roger. 'You're starting in the wrong place. All genealogists (people who study family history) must start with the people they know most about: themselves. You have to make the trunk of the tree *before* you try to find out details about any of the branches. I'll help you if you like. I've always meant to do our family tree.'

So Sophie found a notebook and, under the two headings 'Sophie' and 'Ben', they jotted

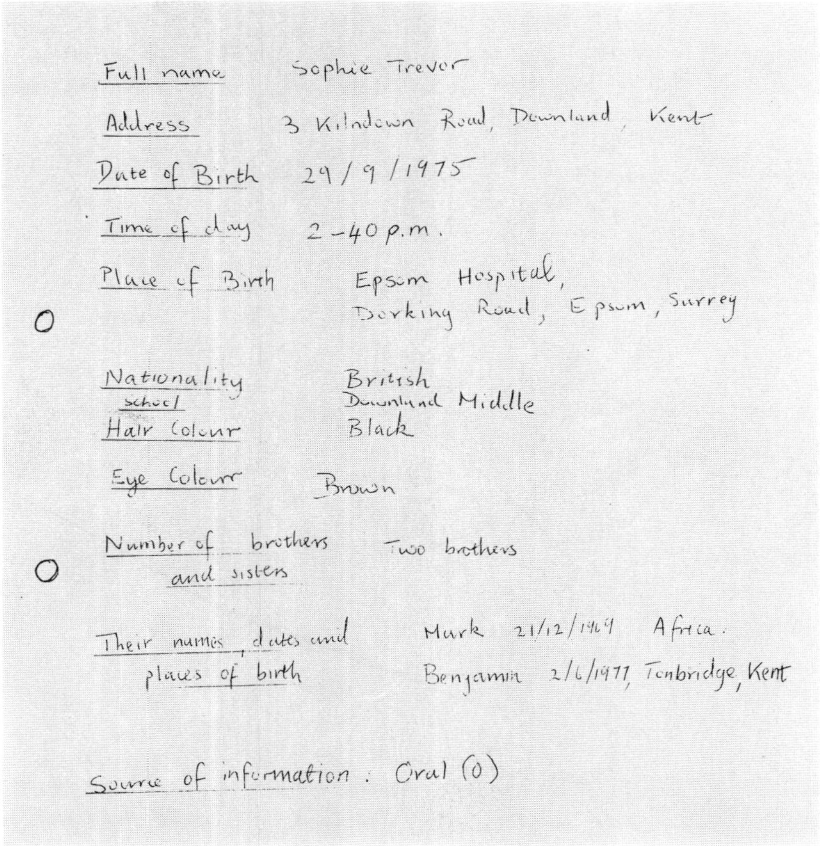

Full name: Sophie Trevor

Address: 3 Kilndown Road, Downland, Kent

Date of Birth: 29/9/1975

Time of day: 2-40 p.m.

Place of Birth: Epsom Hospital, Dorking Road, Epsom, Surrey

Nationality: British

School: Downland Middle

Hair Colour: Black

Eye Colour: Brown

Number of brothers and sisters: Two brothers

Their names, dates and places of birth: Mark 21/12/1969 Africa. Benjamin 2/6/1977, Tonbridge, Kent

Source of information: Oral (O)

When she had transferred her notes to the Family History Book, Sophie's page looked like this.

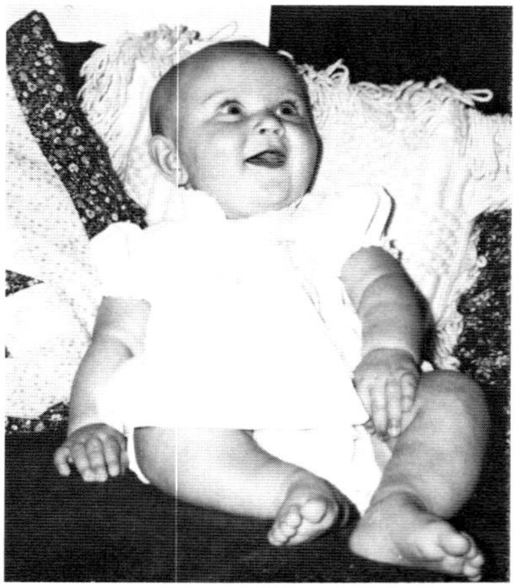

Sophie as a baby.

down everything they knew about themselves. They asked their mother where they were born, and if she remembered at what time of day.

Uncle Roger suggested that they should later transfer their notes into a proper Family History Book, with a page for each person they discovered. A ring binder would be best for this, because its looseleaf pages could be shuffled around as more information came to light.

Next, Sophie and Ben rummaged through the family albums and asked their parents if they might remove a few photos of themselves. They slipped these into plastic wallets and filed them in their ring binder. One or two photos were too big, but with their parents' permission they could usually trim off the edges without losing anything that mattered.

Uncle Roger said that many genealogists try to discover something about the period in which their ancestors lived. They like to know what type of clothes people wore, what sort of transport they had, what their houses looked like, and what kind of furniture was inside. They also find it interesting to read up about historic events that members of their family had lived through.

'You two could make a start by discovering what life was like in the 1970s, when you were born,' he suggested.

Sophie took this snapshot of their home for the Family History Book.

Ben bought a postcard of the area where they lived.

Finding out about the 1970s

Ben and Sophie went to the library and asked the librarian to help them find books on the 1970s. First they made notes about what life was like, and put them in the Family History Book. Then they traced or photocopied pictures of clothing, houses, and other things from the 1970s. They filed these in the Family History Book, and coloured them in.

They discovered that, because the 1970s were not very long ago, life was fairly similar to the present day. People were prosperous, though there were continual strikes. Many railway lines had been discontinued, but faster inter-city trains were running on many main routes.

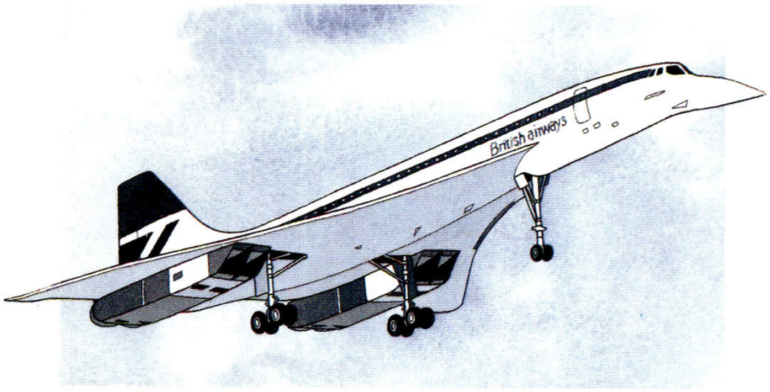

Concorde was the first commercial passenger plane to fly faster than the speed of sound. Jumbo jets travelled more slowly, but could carry lots of passengers cheaply, so many people were able to take holidays in distant places for the first time.

There was a fashion for women to wear long, flowery dresses with dangly beads, even when going to work. They topped their long, flowing hair with floppy, 'garden-party' hats.

New houses in the late 60s and 70s often imitated styles of 200 years before. These brick-built, mock-Georgian buildings had small-paned windows, often set in a bow, and decorative pediments over their front doors.

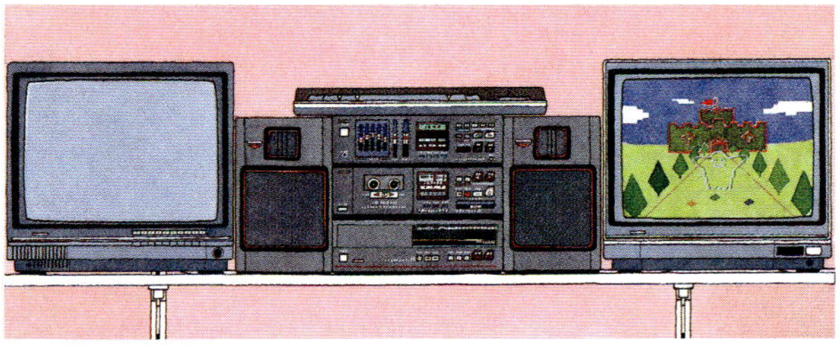

By the 70s home entertainment was very popular. Most families owned a colour television. Music centres were developed to play records and cassettes. Towards the end of the period, home computers were introduced for both games and learning.

The Americans and Russians sent many astronauts into space. Communications satellites circled the Earth to transmit television pictures and telephone calls.

Events of the 1970s

Britain's coinage went decimal – changed from pounds, shillings and pence (£sd) into pounds and (new) pence (£p).

Britain became a member of the European Economic Community (the Common Market).

Queen Elizabeth II celebrated her Silver Jubilee after reigning for twenty-five years.

Margaret Thatcher became Britain's first woman Prime Minister.

Britain and several other countries built platform drilling rigs in the North Sea to extract the oil and gas there.

The world of the 1960s

Sophie and Ben's older brother, Mark, was born in the 1960s, so they found out about that decade too. (A decade is a period of ten years, for example 1970–1980.)

This decade was nicknamed the 'Swinging Sixties' because Britain led the world in young people's fashion and pop music (through groups like the Beatles). It was also called the age of the 'permissive society' – a dramatic change in attitudes to morality, especially among young people. Hippies (or 'flower children') believed the world could exist on a diet of peace and love, and there were 'Ban the Bomb' protest marches against nuclear weapons.

A new design of small motor car was christened the Mini – easy to manoeuvre through the ever-increasing traffic. Giant lorries called juggernauts were developed to transport heavy goods. 5,000 miles of unprofitable railway track were axed, and the first motorways were built.

Hovercraft (invented at the end of the previous decade), cross-channel ferries, and package air holidays introduced many people to continental holidays for the first time.

High-rise 'tower blocks' replaced streets of smaller city houses. Suburban homes were built with large 'picture' windows, open-plan interiors, and front gardens.

Events of the 1960s

A Russian became the first man in space, and two Americans were the first to land on the moon.

The Vietnam War (in which the Americans fought to prevent the spread of communism in SE Asia) ended with the defeat of South Vietnam.

The death penalty was abolished in Britain.

The Berlin Wall was built to separate East and West Berlin.

The 'troubles' (between Catholics and Protestants) flared up yet again in Northern Ireland.

For the first time for over 200 years, men grew their hair long, and clothing became much less formal. The women's liberation movement aimed for greater equality of the sexes, so many men took a greater share of housework, child care, and shopping in the newly introduced self-service supermarkets.

The 60s was the era of the mini skirt, when girls raised their hemlines higher than ever before. Kinky boots or tights were introduced to 'bridge the gap' – instead of the draughty stockings previously worn. Hair was either long and straight, or cut into short, geometrical designs.

Mum's story

When Sophie and Ben had done all they could on their own family history pages, Uncle Roger said they could go on to the next stage.

'But only make one step at a time,' he said, 'and always work backwards. Family historians should never choose a person from the past who has their surname, and try to work forwards to themselves. That person *might* be related, but to prove it, as all good detectives should, they must check very thoroughly through all the linking clues. So, now you must go and find out about the next generation to yourselves (your parents) and then work backwards from there.'

'What's a generation?' asked Ben.

'I know,' said Sophie, 'it's people on the same level of a family tree. You and I and Mark are one generation, Mum and Dad the one before, and our grandparents the one before that.'

'Let's find Mum and Dad!' said Ben.

Mum was digging the garden. 'We want to do your page of our Family History Book next,' said Sophie. 'Have you got time to help us right now?'

'Yes, if you like,' her mother decided, 'I could do with a break from this digging! What do you want to know?'

'Your full name, for a start,' said Sophie.

'Elizabeth Katherine Trevor,' replied Mum. 'Katherine was my mother's and grandmother's name. In the first half of this century, babies were often given their mother's or father's first name as a second name.'

'*I'm* not Sophie Elizabeth,' pointed out Sophie.

'No, it's not so common these days. My maiden name was Grant, just like Grandpa and Grandma G's,' Mum went on. 'A maiden name is the surname a woman is born with. I was Elizabeth Katherine Grant before I married your Dad.'

It hadn't occurred to Ben that Mum's surname had ever been anything but Trevor, but he decided to keep quiet. Mum told them that she was born in York on 24th January, 1950, and attended Stonegate School for Girls. In those days, nearly all secondary schools were either for all girls or all boys.

Mum left school at sixteen and trained for a year as a secretary. She then worked for another year for an engineering company, where she met Dad. He was going out to Africa to advise on the building of a dam. Mum didn't want to be left behind, so they got married in Harrogate on 24th

Mum unearthed some old photos. Sophie and Ben had a good laugh at this picture of her as a baby.

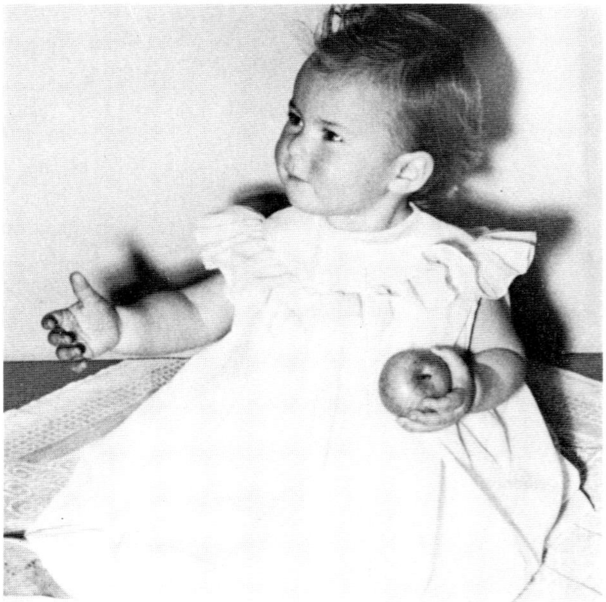

June 1968. They went to Africa together, and Mark (Sophie and Ben's elder brother) was actually born out there.

Mum stayed at home to look after her children until Ben started school, and then she went back

Mum playing on her tricycle.

to work again as a secretary (the job she was still doing).

Mum gave them one of her old typing certificates for their book. Family historians collect such family documents or make photocopies of them – things like wedding invitations, school reports, war call-up papers, letters, and newspaper cuttings.

Mum in her school uniform.

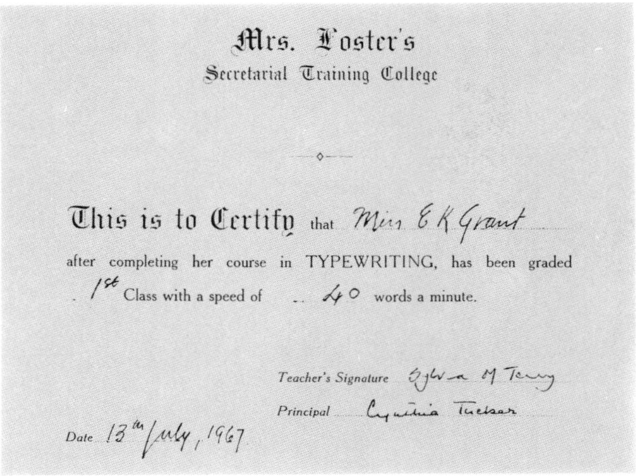

Mrs. Foster's
Secretarial Training College

This is to Certify that Miss E K Grant after completing her course in TYPEWRITING, has been graded 1st Class with a speed of 40 words a minute.

Teacher's Signature Sylvia M Terry

Principal Cynthia Tucker

Date 13th July, 1967

Mum's typing certificate was easy to file in the Family History Book. Objects which can't be put in a book can be stored in a box. Christening mugs, old diaries, school prizes, and pieces of jewellery are all good things to store in such a family treasure chest.

The 1950s when Mum was born

Ben and Sophie researched social history for the decade when Mum was born. They discovered that things were then beginning to brighten up again after the dreary years of the Second World War. The Festival of Britain celebrated progress in art, industry, architecture, and science. Food rationing (a wartime hangover) was finally abandoned in time for the glittering Coronation of Queen Elizabeth II. People earned more money, and spent it on better goods and services than had ever before been available.

War-bombed cities gave town planners an opportunity to improve people's living conditions. Large areas of countryside disappeared

Some young men dressed like this 'Teddy boy' jiving to rock and roll music, and girls wore lots of stiffened, frilly petticoats under bright, very full, circular skirts. Special clothes and record shops, and coffee bars with juke boxes, developed to help teenagers spend their money. Before this, people their age had followed adult fashions.

Jeans and trousers became popular with women and girls. This girl playing with a hula hoop tied back her long hair in a fashionable ponytail. Her home was a prefab (a single-storey prefabricated house assembled very quickly to replace war-damaged housing).

beneath concrete and brick, as whole 'New Towns' like Basildon and Harlow were built.

Steam trains were being replaced by diesel or electric ones, and trams by buses. The Comet, the first passenger jet plane, took to the air, and some tourists made cheap flights to Spain and France. However, most people still holidayed by the sea in Britain, often staying at the developing holiday camps.

Dresses generally were full-skirted and calf-length, with nipped-in waists and many bows. These very feminine fashions were a reaction against wartime utility ones, and were called the New Look. And nylon stockings and underwear had arrived!

Events when Mum was little

In the Korean War, North Korea was supported by China and South Korea by the United Nations.

The summit of Mount Everest was reached for the first time by New Zealander Edmund Hillary and Nepalese sherpa Tenzing Norgay.

Queen Elizabeth II succeeded her father George VI on the throne.

The Suez Crisis: Egypt nationalised the Suez Canal, prompting Britain, France, and Israel to invade.

The Russians suppressed the Hungarian Uprising against communist rule.

The first space flight was made – by an (unmanned) Russian spacecraft (Sputnik).

For the first time ever, a mile was run in under four minutes (by Roger Bannister).

Few people owned a television, but Mum's parents had avidly watched Elizabeth II's coronation on a set bought specially for the occasion.

People became mobile again after wartime petrol rationing was discontinued, and millions bought their first family car. Mum remembered the excitement when her father brought home their first small saloon – a Morris Minor.

All about Dad

Next Sophie and Ben found Dad up a ladder, fixing the leaky gutter. When they asked if he would tell them about himself for the Family History Book, he was very grumpy. Too late they remembered Uncle Roger's advice that they should always choose a tactful moment to ask questions about family history.

By tea-time, Dad had calmed down and was happy to talk. His full name was Andrew Richard Trevor (Richard was his father's second name too) and he was born on 3rd of February, 1940 (the year after the Second World War started).

Although he had been very young, Dad did remember a little about the war. Instead of going to bed at home, he and his family often slept in the air-raid shelter dug in the back garden, while enemy planes droned overhead. Every night, the windows of their house were covered in black-out material so no glimmer of light could make it a target for the bombers.

Food was rationed, so when Dad had a birthday party, his mum saved up sugar, jam, and dried egg for weeks beforehand to make as many nice cakes as possible. Nobody could get bananas during the war, and Dad vividly remembered eating his first one ever when peacetime came. He never tasted an ice-cream until he was seven years old.

Clothing was rationed too, so most wartime clothes had to be home-made. And most toys

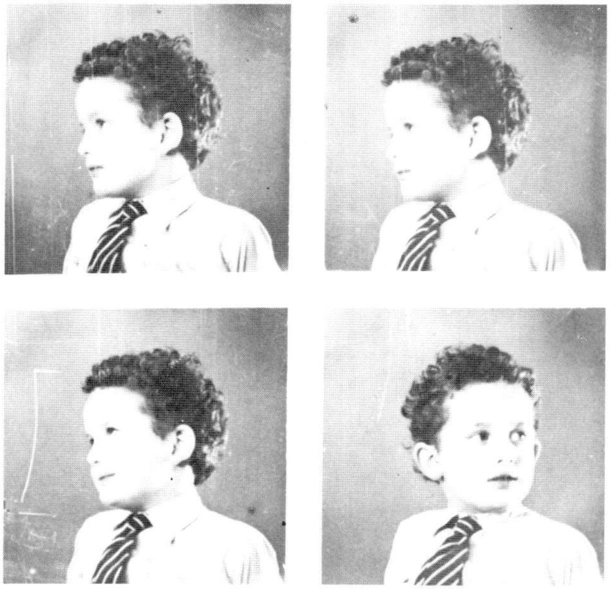

Dad as a small boy.

Dad's brother Micky, who was killed in the doodlebug disaster.

Mum and Dad's wedding photo.

were either wooden, or soft, cuddly ones, because metal was needed for guns and planes.

Dad's worst memory of the war was a very terrible one. In 1944, when rocket bombs (nicknamed doodlebugs) whined overhead, one actually fell on a shop where his mother and his little brother Micky had been queuing for hard-to-get groceries. The shop was flattened and his mum, Micky, and everybody else in it, were killed. Dad remembered the date as the 20th of July. Micky would have celebrated his second birthday on the 29th of September that year.

'How awful!' exclaimed Sophie. 'Was your dad killed too?'

'No, he was away fighting as a soldier,' said Dad, 'and that meant there was no one to look after us children. So we all went to Wales to stay with Auntie Hurst, my mother's sister. We lived with her and Uncle Hurst for the rest of the war. My father came home for the first time early in 1946. He had been away so long that he was a complete stranger to me. I think he felt my aunt and uncle were more our parents than he was, and it would upset us too much to move us away. He decided to emigrate to New Zealand.'

'So your auntie really brought you all up?' said Sophie.

'Yes,' said Dad, 'and I called you after her. Her first name is Sophie too.'

'So I *am* named after somebody after all!' Sophie was pleased.

'What about me?' asked Ben peevishly. 'I'm not named after Dad – or anybody! I wish I could find another Ben Trevor in the family tree.'

'Well,' said Dad, 'hunt long enough, and perhaps you will.'

Andrew Richard Trevor (Dad)
b 3/2/1940 in Dulwich, London
Engineer
= Elizabeth Katherine Grant (Mum)
b 24/1/1950 in York
Secretary
m 4/6/1968 in Harrogate

Mark Trevor b 21/12/1969 in Africa	Sophie Trevor b 29/9/1975 in Epsom, Surrey	Benjamin Trevor b 2/6/1977 in Tonbridge, Kent

Uncle Roger helped Ben and Sophie set out the beginning of their family tree like this. Some of the rules to remember are:

1. *Put youngest generation at bottom of page.*
2. *For brothers and sisters, put eldest on left, youngest on right.*
3. *Keep people of same generation level with each other.*
4. *Put husband and wife side by side, with linking sign (=).*
5. *Include basic information only, e.g. dates of birth (b), marriage (m), and death (d), and occupations where you know them.*

The 1940s when Dad was born

The Second World War, when Dad was little, affected civilians more than any war before or since. Many families were split up. Fathers went off to fight, and children were evacuated to safer parts of the country, clutching their suitcases and gas masks, and wearing identity labels.

At the approach of an air raid, the sound of the warning sirens made people hurry into air raid shelters until the 'all clear' siren let them know it was safe to come out. Uncle Roger told Sophie and Ben that schoolchildren even did lessons underground while enemy aircraft moaned overhead and bombs came crashing down.

But, despite all the hardship and fear during wartime, there was a great sense of community spirit. People helped each other in all their troubles.

Victory, when it came in 1945, was a time of great excitement and celebration. However, rationing of food continued for several years, and the shortages were aggravated by cold winters and power cuts.

While men were away fighting, women took over many of their jobs. They worked in aircraft and munition factories, as bus conductors, and on the railways. Working women often wore trousers (not worn much before) and headscarves instead of hats.

Many people, like this gent in his double-breasted suit and homburg hat, came home in the evening to find their home had been bombed flat! Men like Andrew Trevor's Uncle Hurst, who were too old to be called up into the forces, joined the part-time Home Guard ('Dads' Army').

Everybody had a ration book and could only buy as much food as they had coupons left in it. At one stage the egg ration for an adult was only one a fortnight! Babies like Andrew and Michael Trevor received extra vitamins, orange juice, and dairy foods. Clothing, petrol, sweets, and furniture were also rationed.

MINISTRY OF FOOD

RATION BOOK

OFFICIAL PAID

HOLDER'S NAME AND REGISTERED ADDRESS

Compare with your Identity Card and report any difference to your Food Office

Surname SMART

Other Names Janet

Address 4 Oak St. London W3

DO NOT ALTER

ISSUED JULY 1942

NATREG NUMBER SSFS 76 2

SERIAL NUMBER OF BOOK

If found return to Ealing FOOD OFFICE

RR 918497

R.B.1 General

1942-43 CLOTHING BOOK

This book may not be used until the holder's name, full postal address and National Registration (Identity Code) Number have been plainly written before IN INK.

NAME Janet Smart

ADDRESS 4 Oak Street

(TOWN) London W3

NATIONAL REGISTRATION (IDENTITY CODE) NUMBER

SSFS / 76 / 2

N. H. M.F.

Events when Dad was young

British and French troops retreating from the Germans were rescued at Dunkirk by the Royal Navy and a fleet of privately owned 'little ships'.

Princess Elizabeth and Lieutenant Philip Mountbatten (later the Queen and the Duke of Edinburgh) were married, and Prince Charles was born.

The Welfare State and the National Health Service were introduced, and Britain's basic industries (coal, steel etc) were nationalised.

India was separated into two countries – India and Pakistan.

Several countries of eastern Europe came under Russian communist control; and China became a communist republic.

About half of Palestine came under Jewish control as the new state of Israel.

Ships bringing food to Britain were liable to attack by German submarines. Therefore Britain imported only essentials, and parks and gardens were used for growing vegetables. Thousands of women ('land girls') took men's places on the farms, using tractors like this one with no protection against noise and weather.

Going sideways – aunts and uncles

When Ben and Sophie came to transfer their notes to Dad's page of their Family History Book, they realised that they had forgotten to ask him *where* he was born, and had to disturb him again.

'Look,' said Uncle Roger, 'I'll make you out a checklist of essential family history questions. If

Auntie Julie pushing a toy dog on wheels. The coat and leggings are very typical of the period.

1 The full name of the person and their relationship to you.
2 Dates (exact or approximate) of births, marriages and deaths.
3 Names and approximate ages of the person's children.
4 Occupations (people may have done several different kinds of job during their lives).
5 All the places where they lived, including addresses of any relatives who are still alive.
6 Any family 'papers' or photographs that might be useful.
7 Any traditions about the family's origins, e.g. that a great-grandfather came from Dorset, or any other anecdotes.

The checklist for interviewing relatives. A portable cassette recorder is useful, though it may put some of your 'victims' off!

Auntie Julie and Uncle Roger at the seaside in 1946. Boys wore short trousers until they were about 12. Girls wore waisted dresses from the 1930s to the 1960s.

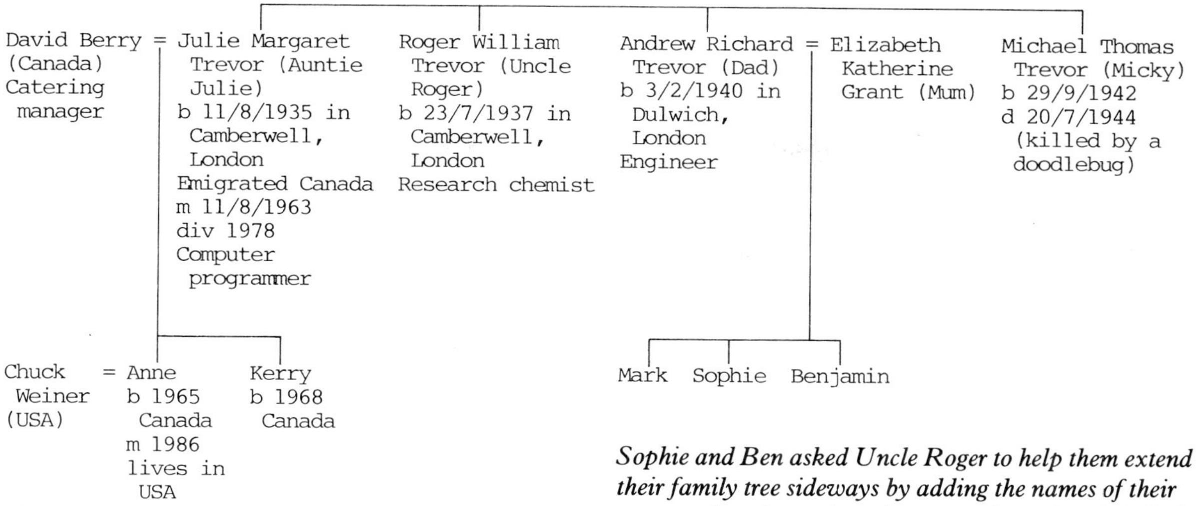

Sophie and Ben asked Uncle Roger to help them extend their family tree sideways by adding the names of their aunts and uncles and cousins – not forgetting their little Uncle Michael who was killed by the doodlebug.

Family trees can get very 'wide' as brothers and sisters spread generations sideways. Keep them narrower by making entries deep rather than broad.

you tick off each one as you get the answer, you won't forget anything. Remember, people may not always tell you the right dates and names, especially when you interview elderly relatives whose memories may be patchy. But their oral (spoken) information gives you a starting point to check later in official records. Also, talking to several relatives about the same thing may help to give a clearer picture.'

'Well, we've more or less "done" Mum and Dad,' said Sophie, 'what do we do next?'

'Either go back another generation and find out about your grandparents,' said Uncle Roger, 'or go sideways and interview other people in your parents' generation.'

'Who do you mean?' asked Ben.

'Your parents' brothers and sisters,' said Uncle Roger. 'Me for a start! I'm your father's elder brother, and Auntie Julie in Canada is his sister. Your mother is an only child, but you can fill in quite a lot about Auntie Julie and me.'

Ben quickly got out a pencil and his notebook, and started to ask questions from the checklist.

Uncle Roger told him that his full name was Roger William Trevor and he was born in 1937 in Camberwell, London. He went to the same school as Dad, and then on to study chemistry at London University. He now worked as a research chemist. He wasn't married.

'You'll have to write to Auntie Julie. Far too expensive to phone Canada,' he said.

So, with a bit of help, Sophie wrote a letter. Auntie Julie wrote back very quickly and sent them some photos. She was born Julie Margaret Trevor, on the 11th of August 1935, in Camberwell. She had emigrated to Canada in 1959 and married David Berry, a catering manager, on her birthday in 1963. They had two children, Anne (b 1965) and Kerry (b 1968) – Sophie and Ben's cousins. Auntie Julie and Uncle David were divorced in 1978, and she now worked from home as a programmer for a computer company. In 1986 Cousin Anne married an American called Chuck Weiner and went to live in the USA.

Uncle Roger suggested it would be fun to pinpoint on a map where everybody in the family lived.

The 1930s when Uncle Roger was born

Uncle Roger and Auntie Julie were born in a time of great poverty and unemployment for many people. This very grim period of the 1930s was called the Great Depression, and more or less swept away the gaiety of the 1920s.

Despite the poverty, many homes were built for the middle classes in the newly developed outer suburbs. Speculative builders hurriedly constructed thousands of semi-detached houses. A few houses were built in the curved 'Odeon' style, often of concrete and with flat roofs.

The popular entertainment of the period was going to the cinema. Hollywood produced a stream of dazzling films whose stars were fêted round the world. Mickey Mouse and Donald Duck were born!

Most people got about on buses, trams, and electric trolley buses. Cars were now usually closed in, instead of being open-topped as in previous decades.

Millions of people found themselves out of work. Particularly hard hit were the shipyard workers in the north of England at Jarrow, and many of them set out for London on protest 'hunger marches'.

Not everybody was hard up. Smart women dressed in a very slinky and elegant fashion, with long clinging skirts, small tip-tilted hats, and fox-fur wraps. Small boys wore grey suits with short trousers, long socks, and caps, a style which lasted for decades.

There was a fashion for mock-Tudor houses. Even semi-detached houses were given bay windows with diamond-shaped panes, and had blackened planks of wood stuck on their outside gables to look like beams.

Events of the Thirties

The collapse of share values on the American stock market led to the 'Depression' in America and Europe.

Adolf Hitler came to power in Germany, and began to prepare the country for war.

King Edward VIII succeeded his father George V; abdicated the throne in order to marry American divorcée Mrs Simpson; and was in turn succeeded by his brother George VI.

The defeat of the Republicans in the Spanish Civil War brought General Franco to power.

World War II began with Germany's invasion of Poland.

The period of the 20s and 30s was the heyday of the luxury passenger ships. The liner Queen Mary, *launched in 1934, was the high point of British shipbuilding. In 1936 she captured the coveted Blue Riband trophy for the fastest transatlantic crossing.*

Mum's parents – Grandma and Grandpa G

'Now you really *can* go two steps back, to your parents' parents,' said Uncle Roger, after Sophie and Ben had completed their 30s material. 'Your Mum's parents (Grandma and Grandpa G) should be easiest, because they live nearby. But do telephone or write to them first to warn them what you want. You should always do this, so your relatives have time to think about what they can tell you. Perhaps they will dig out their old photograph albums and family papers for you to look at.'

Grandma G as a small girl with her mother, who is wearing a typical pull-on cloche hat of the 1920s.

Grandpa G as a schoolboy. Caps were always *worn to go to school, and outdoors generally.*

So Sophie and Ben interviewed Grandma G with their checklist of questions. She was born Katherine Eileen Stokes on 10th July, 1924 in Ripon. She remembered a visit to London, standing in a crowd to cheer King George VI and Queen Elizabeth (later the Queen Mother) after their Coronation in 1937.

Katherine Eileen Stokes and William Eric Grant on their wedding day. Material was very scarce during the war, so her wedding dress is fairly plain. Often brides got married in a plain suit.

Grandma G also talked about her one and only doll, which had a beautiful porcelain face. It was so precious that she was only allowed to play with it on Sundays. One boring, rainy Wednesday, she sneaked the doll out of the glass cabinet in which it was kept and accidentally dropped it. She had to stand in the corner of the room as a punishment.

Grandma G left school at sixteen. Her first job was as a doctor's receptionist. During the Second World War she served in the Wrens (Women's Royal Naval Service) and met Lieutenant William Grant, a soldier.

They managed to wangle leave at the same time after the war ended, and got married on 5th April, 1946. They were both demobbed (released from military service) later that year, and their child Elizabeth (Ben and Sophie's mother) was born in 1950.

Like many women of her time, Katherine did not work at a job outside the home after she married. She now did voluntary work running 'Meals on Wheels' to the elderly.

Ben thought Grandma G was old enough to have 'Meals on Wheels' herself, but thought he had better not say so!

Grandpa G said he was born in 1920 in Aylesbury, Buckinghamshire. As a boy, he loved playing with his Meccano construction kit and Hornby clockwork train set. He was rather naughty at school and got caned a lot. His first job was as a junior clerk in the Ministry of Agriculture, but when war broke out in 1939 he was called up, and served with the army in Africa and Italy.

After the war, he went back to his old job and ended up as a senior civil servant. He retired in 1980 and now did voluntary work for the handicapped.

William Eric Grant (Grandpa G)	=	Katherine Eileen Stokes (Grandma G)
b 15/9/1920 in Aylesbury, Bucks.		b 10/7/1924 in Ripon, Yorks.
Junior clerk, Ministry of Agriculture		Doctor's receptionist
Lieutenant, Army (Second World War)		Wren (Second World War)
Senior Civil Servant (retired)		m 5/4/1946

Elizabeth Katherine Grant (Mum)

The 1920s when Mum's parents were born

Grandma and Grandpa G were born when people were recovering from the dreadful period of the First World War. In the 20s people with money lived a carefree, butterfly-like existence until the final months of the decade when the collapse of shares on the American stock market (known as the Wall Street Crash) led to world-wide economic depression.

Things were difficult for poorer people. There was a brief postwar boom, then many soldiers who had fought, and even been wounded, for their country found themselves out of work. Workers became so angry at poor wages that they took part in the General Strike of 1926.

Before the First World War the middle classes had always had at least one, and often several, servants. Now they found themselves without any, or with only a daily 'help'. (Women who had enjoyed better pay and friendly company in factories during the war were no longer prepared to endure domestic service.)

Fortunately for their former mistresses, 20s furniture tended to be less fussy than that of the Victorian era, so it was easier to keep clean. Some labour-saving devices had been invented (vacuum cleaners, refrigerators, electric cookers, washing machines and so on) – all powered by the electricity which was finding its way into many homes. But, as Grandma G told Sophie and Ben, these machines were primitive compared to those around today!

Events when Grandpa G was young

Ireland split into the Republic of Eire and the 'Six Counties' of Ulster (Northern Ireland).

The first radio broadcasts were made in Britain.

Millions of workers downed tools in the General Strike of 1926.

The first 'talking' films appeared, with a soundtrack added to previously silent 'moving pictures'.

Charles Lindbergh was the first person to fly the Atlantic solo and non-stop.

Women shortened their skirts to the knee, lowered their waistlines, shingled or bobbed their hair boyishly short, and flattened their figures. Rich girls (like this one dancing to radio music) smoked in public like men, wore make-up, and greatly annoyed their starchy Victorian mothers.

Electric trams were a common form of city transport. They ran on a pair of rail tracks set in the road, and were powered by an electric current flowing down a conductor arm from an overhead wire.

Smart young 20s men sported summer outfits of stripy blazer, light flannel trousers, two-tone shoes, 'straw-boater' hat, cane – and sometimes even a monocle. The Austin 7 car brought motoring within the reach of lots of people.

In the 20s, healthy outdoor pursuits like cycling and rambling became popular. This cyclist wears plus-fours (baggy knee breeches), tweed jacket, and colourful knitted pullover. Smoking was considered manly, with no suggestion of the health hazard we now know it is.

Dad's parents – Granny and Grandad Trevor

Granny Elsie Trevor, Great-aunt Sophie, and their brothers, in about 1916. Buttoned boots, like those worn by Elsie and her brother Henry, had been worn by children since Victorian times. The frock worn by the youngest, Jimmy, was traditional for small boys until they were two or three years old. The oldest boy, Thomas, has a painfully stiff, starched Eton collar. Many boys from 1860 onwards wore these for school, and for best.

'Dad,' asked Sophie a few days later, 'how can we find out more about *your* parents? Your mother is dead and your father is in New Zealand.'

'Your Great-aunt Sophie Hurst is the person you want,' said Dad. 'My mother's sister. We'll go and visit her next weekend.'

Ben asked if a great-aunt was a very big person, but Dad said 'great-aunt' and 'great-uncle' were the names given to grandparents' sisters and brothers. They can often tell you lots about your grandparents, because they knew them when they were young.

Great-aunt Sophie had been living abroad for twenty years, but had recently returned to the very same Welsh village where she brought up Dad, Auntie Julie, and Uncle Roger. She had unearthed her old photo albums for Sophie and Ben's visit.

'I haven't looked at these for years,' she said, turning over the pages enthusiastically, 'so your family tree project gives me a good excuse .... Your grandmother, my younger sister, was born

Great-aunt Sophie. Permanently waved or 'permed' hair was popular in the 1930s.

in 1910 in Blackheath. Her name was Elsie Margot Ainsworth. She was a typist before she got married.'

'When was that?' asked Ben, ticking off points on his checklist. He was finding out that information didn't always come in the order of the list.

'June 1934, I think. I was a bridesmaid, but I can't find the photo of the wedding.'

'Never mind,' said Uncle Roger to Ben and Sophie. 'You'll never get *everything* for your Family History Book. No genealogist ever does.'

'Elsie's husband, your grandfather in New Zealand, should know the exact date,' went on Great-aunt Sophie. So, when they all got back home again, Sophie and Ben wrote him a letter.

Grandad Trevor was delighted to hear from his English grandchildren, and was happy to send his 'details'. He told them that his full name was Richard George Trevor and he was born on 16th February, 1911, in Berkshire. His most vivid childhood memory was of seeing a Zeppelin (a German airship) being shot down in flames during the First World War.

Grandad left school at fourteen. In the 1930s he worked as a shop assistant. He didn't like his job very much, but there were so many unemployed that it was very difficult to change jobs.

In 1939, when the Second World War broke out, Grandad joined the army and spent most of the war in the Far East. After the war, in 1946, he emigrated and found work in a bank. He married again – a New Zealander called Mary Tomkins, a widow with a son called Frank. Later, she and Grandad Trevor had two children of their own. Grandad Trevor became a bank manager, but was now retired. He had three grandchildren in New Zealand.

Grandad Trevor sent this picture of himself and his New Zealand family. From right to left they are: Grandad; his second wife, Mary; Frank, her son by her first marriage; and Sally and Basil, Grandad's children by Mary. Their relationships to Sophie and Ben's father are: father, step-mother, step-brother, half-sister, and half-brother. (The 'half' means one parent is shared but not the other.)

Henry Hurst = Sophie Ainsworth (Auntie Hurst/ Great-aunt Sophie) b 4/11/1906

Thomas Ainsworth b ?1908

Elsie Margot Ainsworth (Granny Trevor) b 4/8/1910 in Blackheath, London Typist m June 1934 d 20/7/1944 = (1) Richard George Trevor (Grandad Trevor) b 16/2/1911 in Berkshire Shop assistant Army, Second World War Emigrated to New Zealand Bank manager (retired) = (2) Mary Tomkins (widow) Australia

Henry Ainsworth b c1912

James (Jimmy) Ainsworth b 1915

Julie Margaret Trevor (Auntie Julie)

Roger William Trevor (Uncle Roger)

Andrew Trevor (Dad)

Basil

Sally

Frank

The 1910s and the First World War

Granny and Grandad Trevor were born in the decade of the 1914–18 war. This 'Great War' was the first to involve the whole world, and it moved Britain from the golden age of the previous Edwardian era (the 1900s) into a much more sombre period.

Most notable was the effect on young men and their families. Men and even boys had enthusiastically volunteered to fight the Germans when war broke out, cheered on their way by an enthusiastic population. But nearly a million Britons were killed in the mud and blood of the trenches in Flanders (Belgium), or choked or blinded with poison gas. It was a war of deadlock, mass slaughter, and of civilian involvement as never before.

This First World War soldier is walking with a lady friend who wears a typical 1910s skirt falling to the ankles. Around 1912 really fashionable ladies wore hobble skirts so tight that they could barely walk.

In America in 1903 the Wright brothers had managed to get the world's first aeroplane off the ground. By the First World War planes were still very flimsy constructions of wood and wire, and their pilots were completely exposed to the wind and rain. Aircraft were used during the war, first for reconnaissance, and later for bombing. By the last year of the war, pilots were fighting each other with machine guns fixed to the aircraft nose.

Before the war some women were energetically campaigning for the right to vote in general elections. They were called suffragettes, but during the war they suspended their campaign to join other women helping with the war effort. They worked as 'clippies' on the buses, ran soup kitchens for the troops, and so on. Women over 30 were rewarded with the vote in 1918, but younger women not until 1928.

Events when Great-aunt Sophie and Granny Trevor were young

King George V succeeded his father Edward VII.

The so-called 'unsinkable' liner *Titanic* did sink, and many people were drownd.

The First World War lasted from 1914 to 1918.

The Easter Rising in Ireland (a nationalist revolt against the British government) was to lead eventually to independence for the Irish Republic.

In the Russian Revolution the Bolsheviks overthrew and murdered the Tsar, and introduced the world's first communist republic.

Two Englishmen, Alcock and Brown, made the first non-stop flight across the Atlantic.

Electric lighting in homes became common during the decade, and many homes boasted telephones from 1911. Great-aunt Sophie remembered there had been one of these candlestick phones at home when she was a girl. It had no dial, as all numbers were obtained by an operator.

Great-grandparents – and a family outing

'You could now go sideways again and find out more about your grandparents' other brothers and sisters,' said Uncle Roger. 'Otherwise, your next job is to go a third step back to your great-grandparents.'

'Were they extra-big people too?' joked Ben.

'Of course not,' scoffed Sophie. 'They are Mum and Dad's grandparents.'

'This is how it works,' said Uncle Roger. 'From now on, each generation will have another 'great' added to it – great-great-grandfather, and so on. Everyone has *eight* great-grandparents, but it is usually difficult to find out as much about them as you've discovered about your parents and grandparents. Often, they will have already died.'

'My mother's mother – your maternal great-grandmother – *is* still alive,' said Mum, who had been listening with interest. 'It's ages since I saw her, but Grandma G sees her quite often.'

So one Sunday they all drove to Lincolnshire to visit their great-grandmother. She was delighted to see them. Always known as Kate, she said her full maiden name was Katherine Vera Markham. She was born on 4th March, 1900, in the same house in the village of Ricking where she still lived. Ben and Sophie were very interested to see the house in which part of their family had lived for several generations.

Like so many young men of their generation, Kate's three elder brothers – Humphrey, Sidney, and Edwin – had all been killed in the mud and blood of the trenches during the First World War.

Great-grandmother Kate Stokes as a little girl nursing her doll.

Great-grandfather Wilfred Stokes. Sailor suits were popular for young boys from Victorian times until the early years of the twentieth century.

Humphrey killed in First World War

Sidney killed in First World War

Edwin killed in First World War

Katherine Vera Markham ("Kate") b 4/3/1900 in Ricking, Lincs. 'Flapper' m 14/2/1923 = Wilfred Burrows Stokes b 3/1/1901 in Selby, Yorks. Car salesman RAF (Second World War) d 10/5/1942 (shot down)

Katherine Eileen Stokes (Grandma G)

'So many families were bereaved like that,' she explained. 'Millions of young men died.' Then she went on more cheerfully. 'I married your great-grandfather, Wilfred Burrows Stokes, in 1923, on St Valentine's Day. He was born in Selby, Yorkshire. I always thought he was older than me, but when he died and I found his birth certificate among his papers, I discovered he was younger. I'll look the certificate out for you. I expect the confusion happened because he lied about his age to try to get into the Royal Flying Corps in the First World War.'

Ben was going to ask what a birth certificate was, when he remembered Uncle Roger's warning against interrupting elderly relatives in the full flow of their memories.

'Wilfred loved fast transport,' continued Great-grandmother. 'After the war he became a salesman for Rolls-Royce cars, and during the General Strike of 1926 he actually drove a train! When the Second World War broke out, he became an observer in a bomber crew. He was shot down over Germany on 10th May, 1942.

Great-grandmother Kate gazed sadly into the distance as she remembered this. Everybody else kept very quiet.

Great-grandfather Wilfred Stokes' birth certificate is the official record of his birth. His parents would have been given a copy. A birth certificate shows a genealogist several useful things.

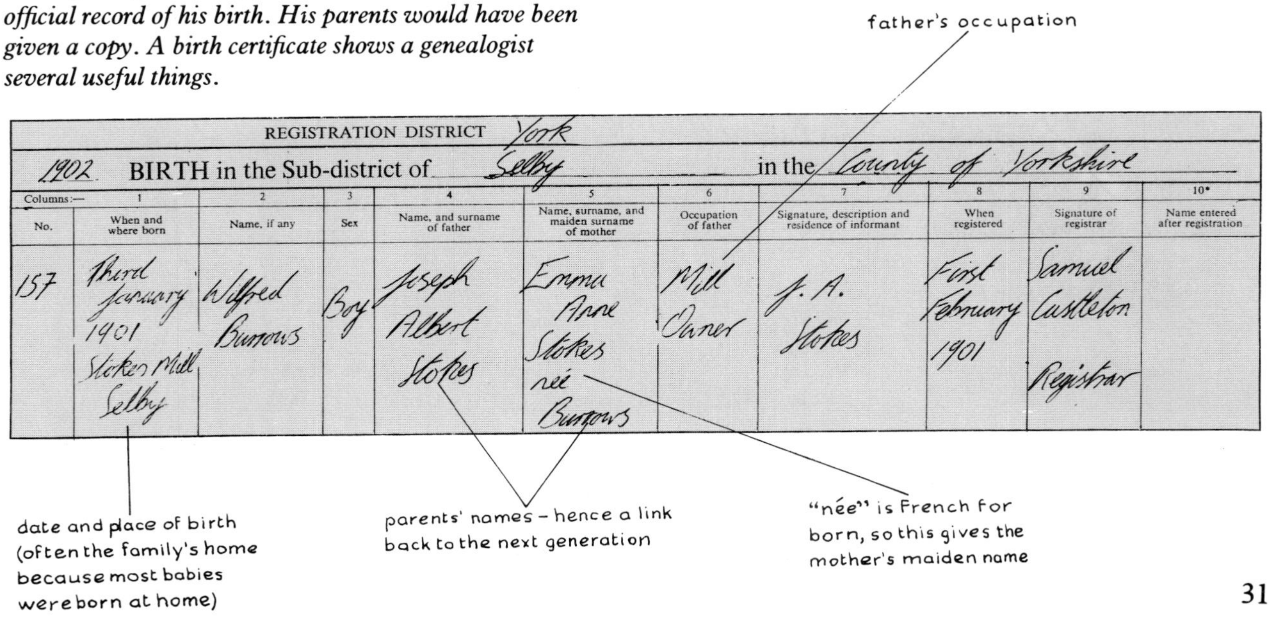
REGISTRATION DISTRICT York

1902 BIRTH in the Sub-district of Selby in the County of Yorkshire

Columns:— 1 When and where born	2 Name, if any	3 Sex	4 Name, and surname of father	5 Name, surname, and maiden surname of mother	6 Occupation of father	7 Signature, description and residence of informant	8 When registered	9 Signature of registrar	10* Name entered after registration
No. 157 Third January 1901 Stokes Mill Selby	Wilfred Burrows	Boy	Joseph Albert Stokes	Emma Anne Stokes née Burrows	Mill Owner	J. A. Stokes	First February 1901	Samuel Castleton Registrar	

The 1900s and the Edwardian era

Great-grandmother Kate Markham grew up during the Edwardian period. Edward VII was on the throne, and high society flourished with lavish and elegant balls, weekend house-parties, shooting, yachting, etc – all supported by hosts of servants.

Even the middle classes had servants. Great-granny Kate said her parents' household included a cook, housemaid, parlourmaid, nurse, nursemaid, and gardener-coachman. Less well-off people were helped by at least one general maid. In fact, domestic service was one of the few careers open to working class girls at that time.

In the streets electric light was fairly common, and Great-granny Kate remembered how everyone stared if they saw one of the rare motor cars. The first aeroplanes also created a sensation, especially as they had to fly quite low, making a stuttering, motor-bike sort of noise.

There was still a lot of poverty at this time throughout the country, and almost one-third of London's population was poor.

Well-to-do Edwardian ladies wore full, trailing frocks with lots of lace, frills, and trimmings. They hauled in their waists with diabolically tight stays (corsets) to give themselves an overall S-shape. Their gigantic hats were weighted down with artificial flowers, fruit, or feathers. This lady is listening to a horn gramophone.

Robert Baden-Powell set up the Boy Scout Movement in 1908, basing its uniform on that worn in South Africa during the recent Boer War. This scout parades in front of a row of terraced houses typical of the Edwardian period, with bay windows, and decorative ridge tiles to their roofs.

Double-decker motor buses appeared in the Edwardian decade, and more and more motor vehicles were seen on the roads, though horses still pulled many buses and trams until the First World War. Great-granny Kate remembered seeing a wonderful mixture of steam, electric, and horse trams jamming the streets.

Events when Great-granny Kate was young

Queen Victoria died after sixty-three years on the British throne, and was succeeded by her son Edward VII.

The Boer War in South Africa ended with defeat for the Afrikaners in their struggle to remain free from British rule.

After years of experiment, the Wright Brothers flew the first aeroplane.

The French pilot Blériot made the first plane crossing of the English Channel.

Australia and New Zealand became independent countries.

The Russo-Japanese war ended in defeat of Russia.

This is the style of dress worn for a family outing in the country by a middle-class man. He is sufficiently well off to afford the expensive hobby of photography. That large camera, tripod, and the heavy glass slides used instead of film, would have needed a motor car to carry them — or at least an extra servant.

The Family Bible

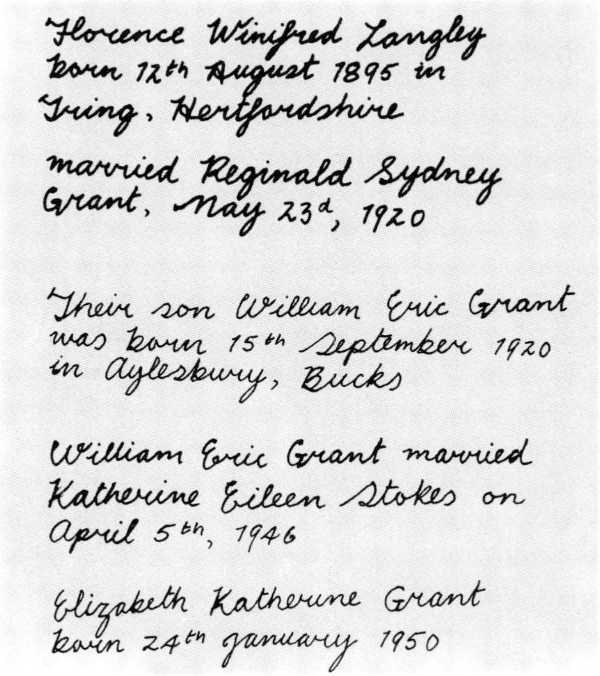
Florence Winifred Langley
born 12th August 1895 in
Tring, Hertfordshire

married Reginald Sydney
Grant, May 23d, 1920

Their son William Eric Grant
was born 15th September 1920
in Aylesbury, Bucks

William Eric Grant married
Katherine Eileen Stokes on
April 5th, 1946

Elizabeth Katherine Grant
born 24th January 1950

Some of the entries in the Family Bible.

'You know that my mother (your Great-grandmother Florence) died recently,' said Grandpa G when Sophie asked him about his parents. 'Well, I've found her Family Bible. That should be useful to you two family tree detectives.'

Out of a drawer he produced a big old black Bible, with a battered and worn cover. A page at the front had funny, old-fashioned, faded writing on it – names of people mostly called Grant, and dates.

'A Family Bible,' Grandpa said, 'was often given to a couple when they got married. In it they recorded the names and dates of birth of their children, and later on their marriages and perhaps even deaths. See, there are my parents' names and . . .'

'Look,' shouted Ben, '*we're* in it as well, Sophie.'

'Yes, my mother kept it up all through her life,' said Grandpa G. 'See, she was born Florence Winifred Langley on 12th August, 1895, in Tring in Hertfordshire. And there's her marriage – to my father, your Great-grandfather Reginald Sydney Grant, just after the First World War. She was a nurse in a military hospital and that's where they met. He was wounded, you know. After he was demobbed, he worked in a shoe factory.'

'But what about the embroidered postcard and the mystery photo in her cabinet?' asked Sophie. 'Your father's name wasn't Hubert!'

Grandpa G rummaged in a big cardboard box. 'Here are some more of my mother's things,' he said. 'See if there are any useful clues there.'

Ben flicked through the pages of a little book.

'That's a birthday book,' said Grandma G, 'for remembering people's birthdays. See, there's an entry on 27th June, for Reg's birthday – luckily, it even gives the year he was born. So you can pencil in 1895 for your great-grandfather's birth and check it later in official records.'

'Here's another date for the tree,' Ben said. 'See, it says: *Reg died 4th November, 1963*. He flicked over some more pages. Suddenly he shouted out, 'Look at this.' Against the date April 1st were the words *Hubert Luker died in 1918. He was killed in action in France age 19. My first love.*

'We've *found* it!' exclaimed Sophie. 'He must be the Hubert of the postcard.'

Great-grandmother Florence Winifred Langley (far right) and some other girls at the seaside. They had to wear their huge, everyday hats even on the beach.

Reginald at school in Birmingham. He is sitting at the right-hand end of the back row. At this period pupils often had to sit with hands behind their backs.

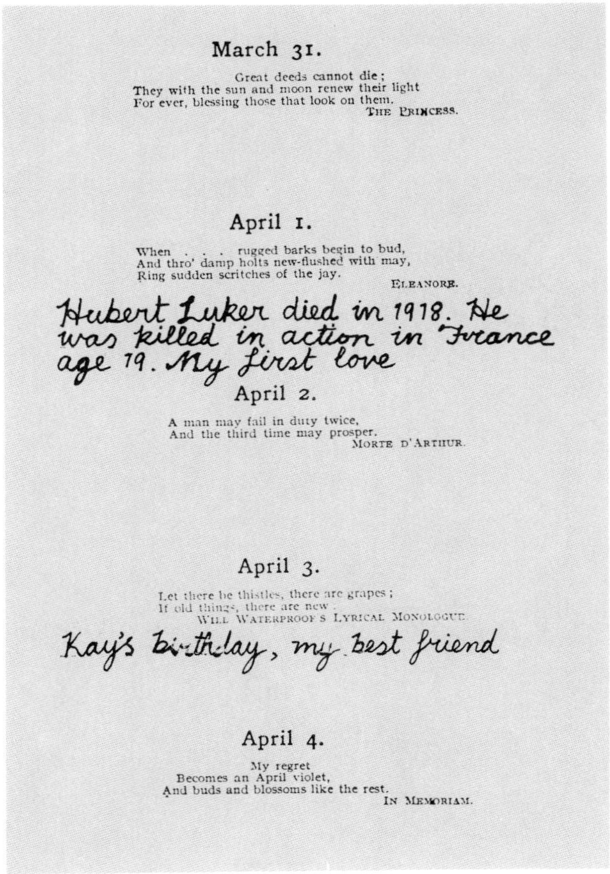

March 31.

Great deeds cannot die;
They with the sun and moon renew their light
For ever, blessing those that look on them.
THE PRINCESS.

April 1.

When . . . rugged barks begin to bud,
And thro' damp holts new-flushed with may,
Ring sudden scritches of the jay.
ELEANORE.

Hubert Luker died in 1918. He was killed in action in France age 19. My first love

April 2.

A man may fail in duty twice,
And the third time may prosper.
MORTE D'ARTHUR.

April 3.

Let there be thistles, there are grapes;
If old things, there are new.
WILL WATERPROOF'S LYRICAL MONOLOGUE.

Kay's birthday, my best friend

April 4.

My regret
Becomes an April violet,
And buds and blossoms like the rest.
IN MEMORIAM.

'Perhaps Florence and Hubert were engaged,' said Grandma G, equally excited. 'Then Hubert was killed and Florence met and married Reg Grant.'

'Very probably,' said Grandpa G. 'Still, we shall probably never know for sure. There are lots of mysteries in most people's lives.'

'We've solved *this* mystery: I'm sure of it,' said Sophie.

'I'll just enter in my mother's death,' said Grandpa G, 'and then you two can look after the Family Bible. You'll be able to make your own entries in it later on, when you get married and have children.'

Sophie and Ben were delighted to have such a great piece of treasure for their collection.

```
Reginald Sydney Grant  = Florence Winifred
 (Great-grandfather)   |  Langley
b 27/6/1895            |  (Great-grandmother)
Soldier in First       | b 12/8/1895 in
 World War             |  Tring, Herts.
Shoe factory worker    | Nurse in First World
d 4/11/1963            |  War
                       | m 23/5/1920
                       | d 27/7/1985
                       |
                       |
          William Eric Grant
           (Grandpa G)
```

The world of the 1890s

The period when Florence Langley was born is nicknamed the 'Naughty Nineties'. Queen Victoria's long reign was drawing to its close, and her son Edward, Prince of Wales (later King Edward VII) was the leader of smart and sometimes outrageous society.

Methods of transport were changing dramatically in this decade. The safety bicycle was invented and looked more or less like bikes today instead of some of the incredible contraptions of the previous few decades. It made cycling a very popular means of transport, giving women, in particular, a new freedom. The first motorbikes were developed, with a top speed of nearly 40 kph.

Motor cars, invented in the 1880s, were still few and far between, and owned only by the well-to-do. Indeed, until the middle of the 90s their speed was controlled by the Red Flag Act. People thought them so dangerous to pedestrians that they had to be preceded by a man with a red flag, to limit their speed to walking pace!

Most of the main railway routes had been opened by the Edwardian era. This locomotive was quite old by that time, but its carriages were typical of the period. Train travel made holidays, and even the occasional day out at the seaside, much easier.

Well-to-do houses had telephones (invented in the 1870s). Some even had internal ones connected to servants' quarters.

Seaside holidays now became popular. Sophie and Ben had a good laugh at snapshots in Florence Langley's family album, and the comic bathing costumes that covered more than they revealed! Bathing machines for changing in were still around.

Fans were a popular feature of evening dress in the 90s. Women had tiny waists (pulled in with stays) above their bell-shaped skirts. Some unfortunate small boys dressed in velvet-and-lace Fauntleroy suits and wore their hair long and curled.

Events of the Nineties

The first silent films were shown publicly (they had pictures but no sound). An atmosphere of suspense or romance was created by a pianist in the hall who played suitable live music to accompany what was happening on the screen.

The Diamond Jubilee celebrated Queen Victoria's 60 years' reign.

The Boer War began.

Commercial gramophone records appeared. They were played through a large horn loudspeaker (see picture on page 32).

Marconi sent the first transatlantic message on radio waves (called wireless telegraphy).

Searching local records

Great-aunt Sophie had filled in a few details about Sophie and Ben's paternal great-grand-parents (her own parents). Her mother had been a suffragette, and had even been put in prison briefly for chaining herself to some railings. Her maiden name was Emily Sophia Hardstone.

'Sophie again!' said Sophie triumphantly.

'*Still* no Ben yet!' grumbled her brother, crossly.

Great-aunt Sophie sent them her parents' marriage certificate. It confirmed Emily Sophia's maiden name, and showed she was 20 when she married Thomas Edward Ainsworth, a solicitor's clerk aged 24, in 1905. Sophie and Ben could therefore look for Emily's birth around 1885, and Thomas's in 1881.

Uncle Roger pointed out how important it was to check all oral evidence with an official record

Thomas and Emily's marriage certificate. Ages may not always be quite correct: people who are still minors (under 21 in those days) and marrying without parents' consent, or who are much older than their partners, might not tell the truth about their ages. Occupations can also be suspect: people can exaggerate their importance. Nevertheless, marriage certificates are extremely useful.

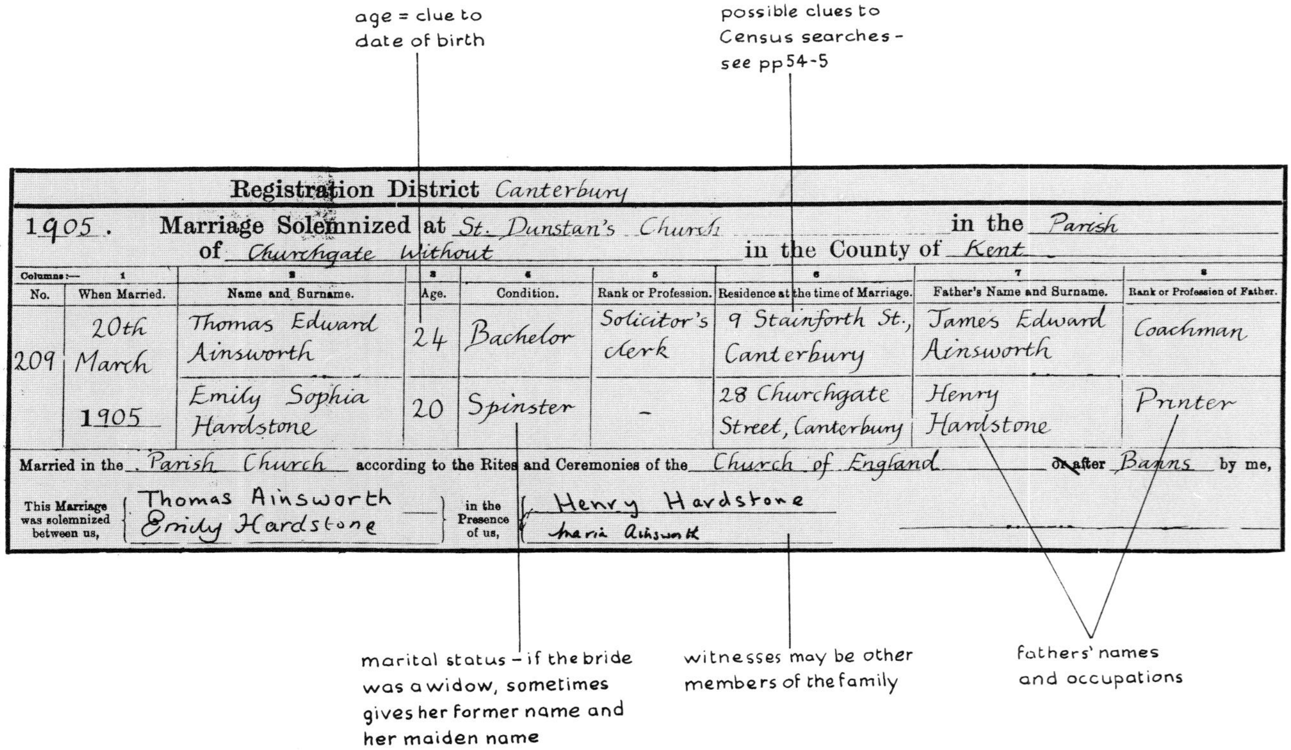

Registration District Canterbury

1905. Marriage Solemnized at St. Dunstan's Church in the Parish of Churchgate Without in the County of Kent

Columns:— 1 No.	1 When Married.	2 Name and Surname.	3 Age.	4 Condition.	5 Rank or Profession.	6 Residence at the time of Marriage.	7 Father's Name and Surname.	8 Rank or Profession of Father.
209	20th March 1905	Thomas Edward Ainsworth	24	Bachelor	Solicitor's clerk	9 Stainforth St., Canterbury	James Edward Ainsworth	Coachman
		Emily Sophia Hardstone	20	Spinster	–	28 Churchgate Street, Canterbury	Henry Hardstone	Printer

Married in the Parish Church according to the Rites and Ceremonies of the Church of England ~~or~~ after Banns by me,

This Marriage was solemnized between us, Thomas Ainsworth, Emily Hardstone; in the Presence of us, Henry Hardstone, Maria Ainsworth

like a marriage certificate. 'People probably won't know *everything* about their relative,' he said, 'or they may even try to hide some family secret from you – like illegitimacy or conviction for trivial crime. Of course, family historians find such fascinating titbits make their ancestors much more like real people!'

'See, Thomas Ainsworth had an office job,' continued Uncle Roger, looking at the marriage certificate again. 'He would have learned to read and write because school was compulsory after 1880. His father was a coachman. He may not have been able to read and write.'

Uncle Roger explained that a marriage certificate was very useful to family historians, providing invaluable information about the couple's occupations and addresses. Often it included their ages – a good clue when looking up their birth certificates. So that seemed to be the next step – to look for Thomas and Emily's births in official records.

Each district keeps the births and deaths for its own area. Luckily, Thomas and Emily had lived in nearby Canterbury all their lives, so Uncle Roger decided first to search its District Register Office records. Sophie and Ben went with him in the car. When they arrived at the Register Office, Uncle Roger paid a rather costly search fee, and they were shown how to look through the indexes. These were a series of hard-cover books filled with handwritten lists of names. Uncle Roger looked for volumes covering the years when Thomas and Emily were likely to have been born.

```
Thomas Edward        = Emily Sophia
 Ainsworth           |  Hardstone
b 3/2/1881 in        | b 28/1/1885 in
 Canterbury          |  Canterbury
Solicitor's clerk    | Suffragette
                     | m 20/3/1905 in
                     |  Canterbury
                     |
                     |
      Elsie Margot Ainsworth
       (Granny Trevor)
```

Thomas Ainsworth and Emily Sophia Hardstone on their wedding day (from Great-aunt Sophie's photo album).

First they looked under 'A' for Ainsworth. It was helpful that both ancestors each had two first names. The records showed several Thomas Ainsworths and two Emily Hardstones, but only one Thomas Edward and only one Emily Sophia. They were born in 1881 and 1885 respectively.

The records clerk at the Office checked these findings by looking in the actual Registers, filled in by hand by the registrar soon after the birth. Thomas's father had not signed his son's birth entry. He had 'made his mark' with a cross because he could not read or write. Uncle Roger's guess had been right.

The world of the 1880s

Sophie and Ben researched the decade when Thomas and Emily Ainsworth were born. They found that by the third quarter of the nineteenth century Britain was nicknamed the 'workshop of the world', because she exported manufactured goods to so many other countries. Starting in Britain a hundred years before, the Industrial Revolution had by the 1880s transformed her industry, helped by plentiful supplies of coal and labour, and also by some brilliant inventors and engineers.

The middle classes now had more leisure than before, and many of them filled it with sporting activities. Cricket became almost a national religion; games were played against Australia, though they were not called 'test matches' until the 90s. Football was still rough and boisterous, but developing into a club and international game; and so was rugby. The average middle class man and woman enjoyed golf, tennis (almost a craze in this decade), croquet, and swimming.

Events of the 1880s

General Gordon was killed at the Siege of Khartoum.

Queen Victoria celebrated her Golden Jubilee (fifty years on the throne).

Girls' public schools gave middle-class girls the same education as their brothers (previously most girls were taught at home, principally domestic subjects).

Dunlop's pneumatic (air-filled) tyre replaced the previous solid rubber, wooden, or iron rims.

A huge volcanic explosion and tidal wave at Krakatoa, Java, drowned nearly 40,000 people.

Things were not so prosperous in the countryside. Farmers in the 80s were in difficulty due to wet seasons in the late 1870s and the importation of cheap American wheat and frozen meat. In fact, farming did not recover from this crisis until the Second World War.

This girl, with her dolls' pram, is wearing a large hat and sailor suit rather like those worn by small boys (see page 30). Her well-to-do parents' house is in a style called Victorian Gothic (embellished with fancy gables, castellated turrets, ornamental stonework, pointed windows, and so on).

Bathrooms were only for the wealthy. Even this luxurious bathroom has no piped water: its bath has to be filled (and its lavatory flushed) from buckets carried up from the kitchen. The ewers (jugs) and basins on washstands (usually in bedrooms rather than bathrooms) were serviced in the same laborious way.

All women, however poor, padded out the backs of their dresses with a bustle, even if made only of newspaper. This fashion lasted from the 1860s to the 1880s. Checked suits had been popular with men since the 1850s, though for formal occasions and at the office frock coats and silk top hats were worn.

Petrol-driven motor cars (called 'horseless carriages') were invented in the 1880s, but it took a long time for them to transform life, especially while they were limited by the Red Flag Act. They were so draughty that ladies had to tie their wide-brimmed hats on with motoring veils. Men wore caped greatcoats to protect themselves against the dust and cold.

The General Register Office

Searching for her Trevor great-grandparents, Sophie had another look at Grandad Trevor's letter. His father William was a carpenter and had fought in the Boer War. His mother Caroline Louisa (née Muir) was a maid. Their golden wedding was in May 1949, so they must have married in 1899. Grandad had no idea when or where either of them was born.

'We'll visit the General Register Office in London,' said Uncle Roger. 'Since 1837 all births, marriages, and deaths in England and Wales have been recorded there. Scottish records are in Edinburgh, those for Northern Ireland in Belfast, and for Eire in Dublin.'

Luckily, it was half-term the following week, so the three of them set off on a day trip to London. Soon they were hurrying through the doors of the Register Office among scores of other family history enthusiasts.

'We'll check William and Caroline Louisa's

Uncle Roger ordered this copy of William Trevor's death certificate to see where *he died, and who reported the death to the Registrar – perhaps a relative. However, death certificates are usually much less useful to genealogists than birth and marriage certificates.*

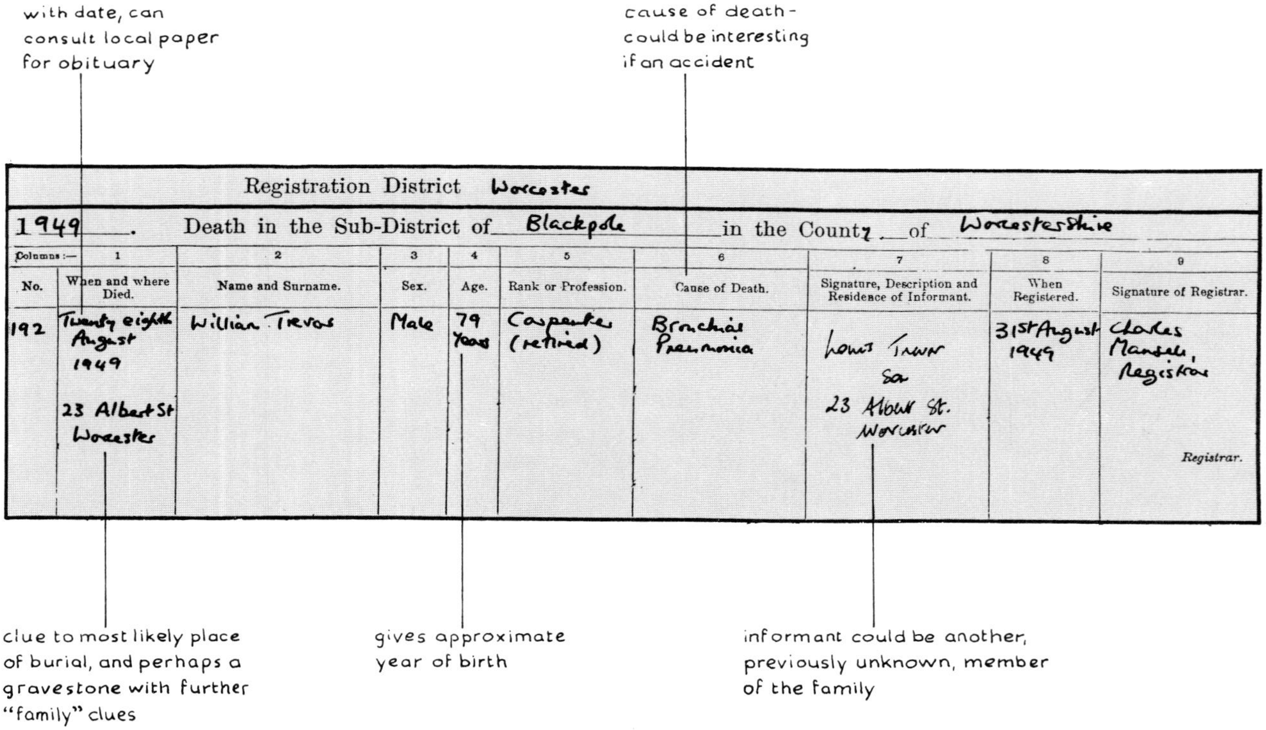
Registration District Worcester

1949. Death in the Sub-District of Blackpole in the County of Worcestershire

Columns:— 1	2	3	4	5	6	7	8	9
No. / When and where Died.	Name and Surname.	Sex.	Age.	Rank or Profession.	Cause of Death.	Signature, Description and Residence of Informant.	When Registered.	Signature of Registrar.
192 Twenty eighth August 1949 23 Albert St Worcester	William Trevor	Male	79 Years	Carpenter (retired)	Bronchial Pneumonia	Lewis Trevor Son 23 Albert St. Worcester	31st August 1949	Charles Mansell, Registrar Registrar.

Great-grandmother Caroline Louisa Muir in her maid's uniform. Perhaps the little child was her employer's daughter.

marriage first,' said Uncle Roger. 'The entries are indexed in three-month periods. As the marriage was probably in May 1899, we'll search the April–June 1899 volume.'

They looked first for Trevor, the less common of the two surnames, heaving down the heavy Index volume marked 'S–Z' and resting it on a long, sloping desk. Eagerly they flipped through the names entered in alphabetical order, and at last they found a William Trevor.

Next they turned to the 'M' Index volume for the same three-month period, to see if Caroline Louisa Muir was there. She was, and the reference numbers were the same, so they knew they had found the right entries. Otherwise, they might have had to search for many years backwards from June 1899, or even forwards in case the marriage was later than Grandad Trevor had thought.

'We'll order a copy of the certificate to check the other information on it,' said Uncle Roger. So they filled in a form, took it to the counter, and paid the clerk.

Their precious certificate could be collected two days later, so on the Thursday up they went again to London. The certificate showed Caroline Louisa Muir's age as 20, but unfortunately William Trevor was described just as 'of full age' – meaning over 21.

Amazingly, Uncle Roger suggested that they should try the *Deaths* Indexes for help with William's date of birth! It didn't take long to track down his death reference, because Grandad Trevor had written that his father had died three months after his golden wedding. The Deaths Index for July–September 1949 reported that William Trevor had died aged 79.

'Who's good at mental arithmetic?' asked Uncle Roger. 'What's seventy-nine years before 1949?'

They thought hard for a while, then Sophie shouted excitedly, 'It's 1870!'

Back they trotted to the Births. There was only one William Trevor born in 1870, in Bristol.

Later they found Caroline Louisa's birth on 2nd November, 1879.

William Trevor	=	Caroline Louisa Muir
b 10/5/1870 in Bristol		b 2/11/1879 in Bristol
Army, Boer War		General maid
Carpenter		m 20/5/1899 in Bristol
d 28/8/1949 in Worcester		

Richard George Trevor
(Grandad Trevor)

The world of the 1870s

Various things were done in this decade to improve the lot of working people, especially children. The horrific practice of using small boys to climb inside and sweep chimneys was banned. The Education Act of 1870 established Board schools, so all children had the opportunity of attending school. (Up to then a few had only a year or so at a dame school run by an old woman before they were set to work in a factory, mine, or on a farm. Or they might just have managed to learn to read and write at a Sunday School, on their only day off each week.

In 1871 the Bank Holiday Act gave all workers six bank holidays a year – previously most had been able to rest only on Saturday afternoons, Sundays, and religious festivals.

After a number of horrifying cholera epidemics, benevolent people felt something had to be done about the insanitary housing of the poor. The Public Health Act of 1875 forced builders to include a lavatory, usually on the ground floor in a lean-to at the back of the house. These outdoor lavatories lasted well into the twentieth century. In his letter to Sophie and Ben, Grandad Trevor recalled how nasty it had been to visit the loo behind his parents' house on a cold, wet, windy night!

Rows of terraced houses were typical of Victorian towns. It was the period of the 'penny farthing' bicycle – nicknamed after a large and small coin of the period. The only way to dismount was to fall off!

Trams, invented in the 1860s, were running well by the 70s. Most were horse-drawn, but some were propelled by steam. They slid easily along rails set in the road. The top deck was open to the weather.

Despite their tightly laced corsets, long skirts with trains, clumsy bustles, and large hats, women actually managed to play some sort of tennis! The modern form of the game developed in the 1870s, with the first Wimbledon championships being held in 1877.

Events of the 1870s

The Franco-Prussian War ended in the defeat of France by Prussia.

The American journalist and explorer H.M. Stanley found the missing explorer Dr Livingstone at Ujiji in Africa.

Voters were allowed to cast their votes secretly. (At previous elections they had to shout out aloud which candidate they voted for, so could easily be intimidated.)

Zulus rose up against the British in the Zulu War.

The first commercial typewriters appeared.

The telephone was invented.

The 'scramble for Africa' began, in which many European countries tried to secure territory there.

Clothes were often made at home. The now widespread sewing machine had been patented by the American Isaac Singer in the 1850s. The lightweight cage on this dressmaker's dummy helped in draping the bustle.

Tombstones and war memorials

Now that they had managed to track down all their great-grandparents, Sophie and Ben wanted to go another step back into the past. Their mother's mother's family looked the easiest, because they could still get some oral information from Great-grandmother Kate Stokes.

Grandma G took them with her on her next visit to Ricking, and Great-grandmother Kate told them that her parents were buried in the local churchyard. In great excitement, Sophie and Ben hurried away to hunt for the grave, remembering they must not run about, shout, or do any damage in such a sacred place. After a long search Ben spotted a grave with the names Great-grandmother Kate had told them.

Great-great-grandfather Robert Markham had died in 1932 aged 67. His wife Lucy Mary Markham had died in 1957 aged 90 (she was the daughter of Frederick Hammond of Grantham). Sophie used her mental arithmetic again, and pencilled in 1865 and 1867 for Robert and Lucy's

Sophie's drawing of Robert Markham's tombstone. According to his daughter, Robert Markham had been the local squire, but family beliefs in rich or famous ancestors should always be checked against written records (discreetly, so as not to upset the teller).

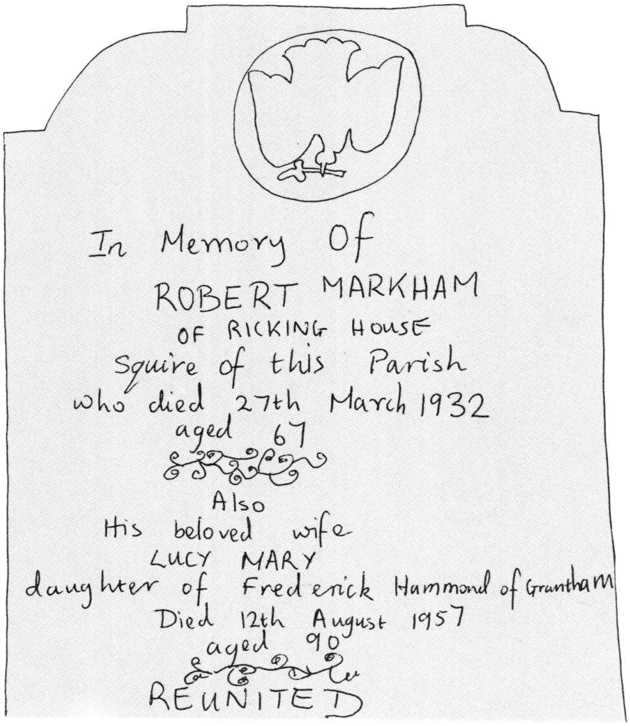

Squire Robert Markham and his wife about 1895 (their style of dress helps to date the picture).

dates of birth, for checking later – ages on tombstones are not necessarily correct.

Nearby Sophie and Ben found some older and very overgrown Markham graves, and copied their inscriptions for future use. Then they went to look at the village war memorial (always worth checking for family surnames). There, among the sad list of First World War dead, were the names of Robert and Lucy Markham's three sons – Humphrey, Sidney, and Edwin. Inside the church was a family monument to them. From the inscription on this, Sophie calculated that the eldest brother, Humphrey, was born about 1892. She planned later to search official records backwards from that date to find Robert and Lucy Mary's marriage.

•

Emma Anne Burrows with her baby. Babies very often wore long clothes.

The birth certificate of Wilfred Burrows Stokes (Great-grandmother Kate's daredevil husband) gave the names of another pair of Sophie and Ben's great-great-grandparents. Wilfred's parents were Joseph Albert Stokes, a mill owner, and Emma Anne Stokes, née Burrows. (Hence Wilfred's second name: it was very common at this time to call children after family surnames.)

The name of Wilfred's birthplace (Stokes Mill, Selby) showed that the mill was probably a family business. Later, searching official records backwards from the date of Wilfred's birth, Sophie discovered Joseph Albert and Emma Anne's marriage in Leeds in 1895. He was 34 and she was 26, the daughter of a clergyman. Joseph was again described as 'mill owner of Stokes Mill, Selby', and his father, Albert Stokes, as 'mill owner (deceased)', which seemed to confirm the family business theory.

Sophie showed the marriage certificate to Grandma G (Uncle Roger had said it was always polite to tell older relatives what they had discovered.) Telling Grandma G had a bonus – it prompted her to rummage in a drawer and produce some very old photos and Emma Anne's certificates from when she was apprenticed as a pupil teacher.

```
Joseph Albert Stokes = Emma Anne Burrows        "Squire" Robert    = Lucy Mary Hammond
(s of Albert Stokes, | (dau of Rev.              Markham of        | (dau of Frederick
 Mill owner)         |  Ernest Burrows,          Ricking House     |  Hammond of
b 1861 in Selby      |  Clergyman)              b ?1865 in         |  Grantham)
Mill owner, Stokes   | b 1869 in Leeds           ?Ricking, Lincs.  | b ?1867
 Mill, Selby         | Teacher                  d 27/3/1932        | m ?before 1892
                     | m 10/9/1895 in Leeds                        | d 12/8/1957
                     |__________                          _________|
                               |                          |
                Wilfred Burrows Stokes = Katherine Vera Markham ("Kate")
```

The world of the 1860s

There was great poverty throughout the whole Victorian period. It was specially bad in the back-to-back slum terraces thrown up hastily decades before, to house workers in the Industrial Revolution.

However, by the 60s when some of Sophie and Ben's great-great-grandparents were born, standards of health care were gradually improving.

Events of the 1860s

Transportation of convicts from Britain to Australia came to an end.

In the American Civil War the Northern states defeated the South, and ended slavery there.

The American President Lincoln was assassinated.

The last public execution was held in Britain.

The Suez Canal was opened.

In Britain the Second Reform Act of 1867 allowed more people to vote, though not yet all.

Diamonds were discovered in South Africa.

Following Louis Pasteur's discovery that disease was caused by bacteria, from 1865 the practice of sterilising equipment, and the use of antiseptics, made operations safer.

After the work of Florence Nightingale in the Crimean War, the standards of nursing and hospital care were vastly improved.

In 1867 Dr Barnardo set up a home to care for destitute children. Over the door was the motto 'No child ever turned away'.

In transport the first horse trams were developed, and also the velocipede ('boneshaker' bicycle) with wooden wheels and iron tyres – the first really practical bicycle. The opening of the first underground railway – the London Metropolitan line in 1862 – greatly eased traffic congestion.

In this decade many of the first underwater cables were laid, to carry Morse telegraph messages. The Great Eastern *was the largest ship built up to that time. It spent much of its time laying cables in the Atlantic, the Mediterranean, and the Red Sea.*

Poor people's houses had no piped water, so whole streets shared a pump. Many destitute children ran about barefoot or in odd, broken-down shoes and ragged clothes. They held horses, swept street crossings free of dust, dirt, and horse droppings, scavenged from river mudflats, or turned to crime – just to exist.

Working and lower middle class families used the kitchen as a living room and kept the parlour for special occasions. The kitchen range heated the room with its open fire, boiled kettles and saucepans on its hob, and baked meat and bread in its side ovens. At bath time a hip bath was placed on the hearth rug and filled with jugs of hot water.

In contrast to the poverty of the streets and slums, the middle classes lived comfortable lives, in stuffy, gloomy rooms with ornate, over-padded furniture and fussy knick-knacks. Men sported curly moustaches, beards, and side whiskers.

Wills and an old jug

'Now for Grandpa G's grandpa!' said Ben, still on the hunt for more great-great-grandparents.

So Grandpa G kindly rummaged again in the effects of his mother, Florence Winifred. '"Effects" is the name for people's possessions when they have died,' he said. 'Ah, here is a copy of my grandfather's will. You can often get lots of family history from wills. You're lucky it's among these papers, because some wills can be quite difficult to track down. I believe all English wills since 1858 are at the Principal Probate Registry in London, but you'd have to look up a specialized family history book for the whereabouts of earlier ones.'

'What *is* a will? asked Ben.

'It's a document which states what a person wants done with his money and possessions when he dies. It gives the name, address, and often the occupation, and usually mentions the wife or husband, the children, and any other people who benefit from the will. Sometimes it refers to the birthplace or the family home or burial place – all very useful genealogical facts.'

The will made by Grandpa G's grandfather linked up some names in the Family Bible which had not meant much before. Sophie and Ben's great-great-grandfather was a Charles Langley of

Extracts from the will of Charles Langley. Perhaps Frederick Welford was Charles's brother-in-law. Ernest Kirkpatrick could also have been a relation by marriage, or just a friend.

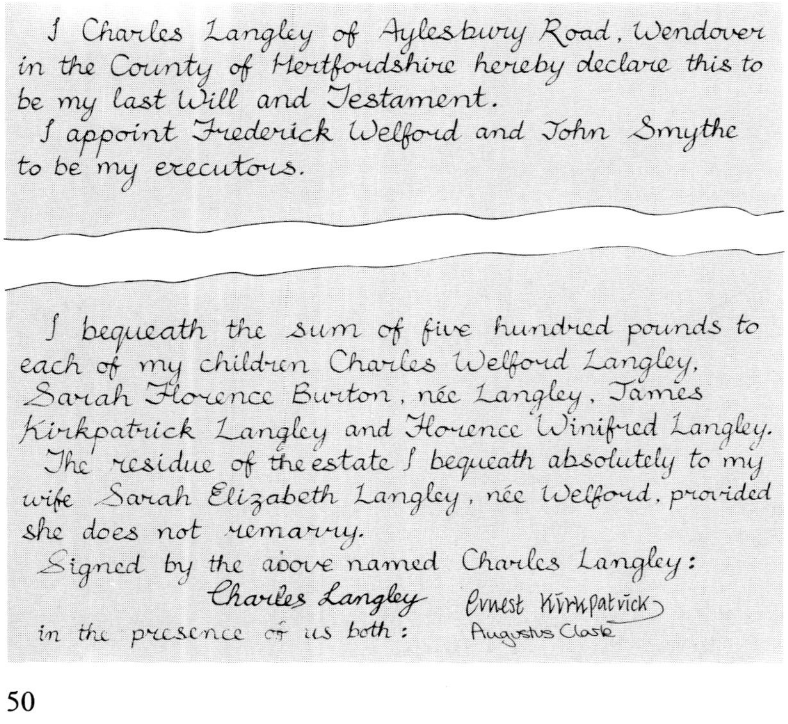

I Charles Langley of Aylesbury Road, Wendover in the County of Hertfordshire hereby declare this to be my last Will and Testament.

I appoint Frederick Welford and John Smythe to be my executors.

I bequeath the sum of five hundred pounds to each of my children Charles Welford Langley, Sarah Florence Burton, née Langley, James Kirkpatrick Langley and Florence Winifred Langley.

The residue of the estate I bequeath absolutely to my wife Sarah Elizabeth Langley, née Welford, provided she does not remarry.

Signed by the above named Charles Langley:

Charles Langley

in the presence of us both: Ernest Kirkpatrick

Augustus Clark

Charles Langley's photo, found among Florence Langley's effects. If the medal can be identified it might reveal interesting facts about army service.

Wendover, Herts. He had a wife called Sarah Elizabeth, and at least four children because they were mentioned in the will. And from the Bible Sophie could also pencil in Charles's date of birth (11th February 1856) and his marriage to Sarah Elizabeth Welford on 23rd April 1885.

That information later led them to a marriage certificate at the General Register Office, which gave them Sarah's age as well as other information they noted down for future use.

•

Grandpa G had also long treasured an old jug with ornamental writing on it. He thought the names on it were those of his paternal grandparents – Henry William and Victoria Fairburn Grant. The inscription indicated that the jug was given to them to mark forty years of marriage in 1919.

The birth certificate, in official records, of Grandpa G's father (Reginald Sydney Grant) confirmed that these people really were Grandpa G's grandparents. Henry William was a shopkeeper and Victoria Fairburn's maiden name was Clark. (Ben also noted that Reginald was born in Birmingham.)

Sophie then took another look at the marriage records for 1879 (forty years before the jug's date). The certificate she found said Henry William was 23, so he was presumably born in 1856. Victoria Fairburn Clark was 21 (born in 1858).

However, Sophie could not find Henry's birth certificate in 1856, so she searched either side of that date and eventually found it in 1859. Evidently, Henry was a minor when he got married, probably without his parents' consent!

Victoria Fairburn Clark. The bustle on her dress suggests the late 1870s or 1880s.

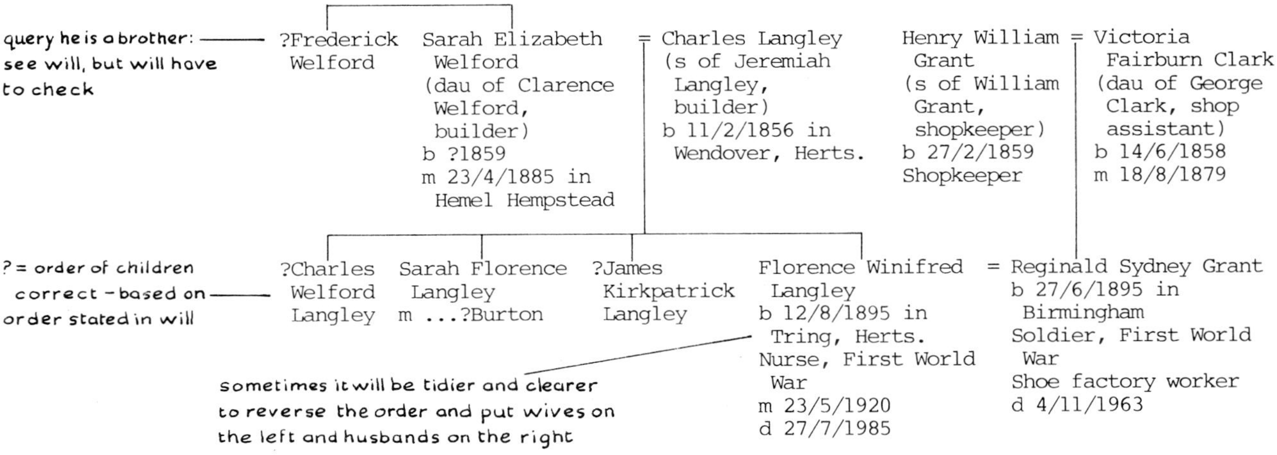

The world of the 1850s

This decade, when Charles Langley and Henry William Grant were born, is often thought of as the heyday of the Victorian period. The Queen had been on the throne twenty years. She and her husband Prince Albert with their nine children set an example of devoted but firm family life which was copied by millions of their middle-class subjects. Going to church, behaviour at meals, paying calls, and receiving guests were all done according to strict disciplined rules.

Trade and industry were prospering, but life was very hard for working people. Men, women, and children worked in factories or mines for twelve hours a day, six days a week, in uncomfortable or dangerous conditions. If they got sick they had to fend for themselves, without free doctors or hospitals. Open sewers ran along streets, and diseases like cholera, typhus, and diphtheria flourished.

Working conditions did improve slightly in the 50s, since it became illegal for children under ten, and for women, to labour in coal-mines; for children under nine to toil in factories; and for children generally to work more than ten hours a day.

Events of the 1850s

The Great Exhibition of 1851 was held in Hyde Park to celebrate British achievement in science and the arts.

Britain, France, and Turkey fought Russia in the Crimean War.

Florence Nightingale improved nursing standards for soldiers in the Crimean War, and began her great campaign for hospital reform.

The Indian Mutiny, an uprising against the British in India, was suppressed, and government of India came under the British Crown.

Work began on the Suez Canal.

The first transatlantic cable was laid.

Well-to-do and even lower-middle-class citizens had servants to keep their large houses clean and to care for their many children. This parlourmaid has a dress puffed out over many petticoats to copy the wealthier women's fashion which was achieved with a cage crinoline.

Ironing the elaborate crinolined dresses of their mistresses was especially difficult for servants before the days of electricity. The charcoal inside the flat iron had to be heated up to just the right temperature, or the dress might be scorched – and the servant sacked!

Coal, essential for heating and cooking in town households, was often tipped down into the cellar through small round 'coalholes' in the pavement outside. Uncle Roger suggested Sophie and Ben looked out for some when next they were in a town.

This two-wheeled taxi, pulled by a single horse and with the driver at the back, was called a hansom cab after Joseph Hansom who invented it in 1834. Its appearance scarcely changed over fifty years. The two passengers got in the front and shut two half-doors in front of them.

Samplers and censuses

'Great-aunt Sophie is your best starting point for *my* maternal great-grandparents,' said Dad. 'I'm sure I've seen a sampler embroidered by her grandmother. Samplers often have names and dates.'

Great-aunt Sophie wrote back that she was sorry she had forgotten to show them the sampler, which had been completed by her grandmother, Mary Ann Body, in 1858, aged 9.

Great-grandmother Mary Ann as a very old lady. Older women wore caps indoors.

Great-aunt Sophie sent this photo of Mary Ann's sampler. Samplers were pieces of embroidery worked by young girls to help them learn needlework.

Sophie and Ben already knew Mary Ann's husband was a Henry Hardstone, because Great-aunt Sophie had given them an *In memoriam* card showing his death on the 31st of December 1892 aged 52.

As a clue to the date of Mary Ann's and Henry's marriage, Great-aunt Sophie thought their daughter (her own mother, Emily Sophia, born 1885) had elder sisters. This seemed likely because she was not named after her mother – from 1600 to 1900 the first two or three children were usually named after their parents or grandparents. Sure enough, it was a very long search backwards from Emily Sophia's birth to her parents' marriage in 1875.

'Family history really *is* like detective work,' said Ben, 'you have to discover the facts you want from the information you already have.'

•

Unfortunately, Great-aunt Sophie knew nothing about her Ainsworth grandparents (another pair of Sophie and Ben's great-great-grandparents). But Uncle Roger examined the family tree and saw that, luckily, their son Thomas Edward (Great-aunt Sophie's father) was born in 1881 – a census year.

'Censuses are very helpful to family historians,' he said.

'What is a Census?' asked Sophie.

'Every ten years since 1801 (except during the Second World War) a National Census has been held. Every householder fills in a form about all the people in the house on Census night, and their relationships to him or her. And each individual's place of birth and age are given. So you know which area to search parish registers and

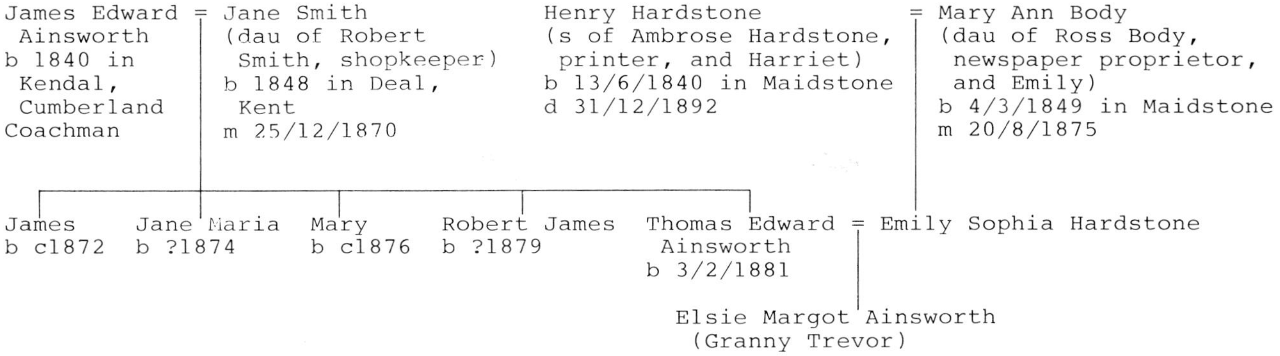

when – essential information before records were kept centrally in 1837.'

'Where can we see a Census?' asked Ben.

'Big libraries often have copies, especially for their particular area. And the whole collection for England and Wales is at the Public Record Office in London,' said Uncle Roger. 'But Sophie and I will have to do that search, because people under 10 aren't allowed in, Ben!'

Thomas Ainsworth's birth certificate gave them the address in Canterbury where his parents were living in 1881 and where he was actually born. With this address, Uncle Roger said they could easily search the 1881 Census for Canterbury.

At the Public Record Office in London, it seemed ages to Sophie before the precious microfilm they wanted was produced. Bursting with excitement, she helped her uncle roll it through a special reading machine, straining her eyes to read the old-fashioned handwriting.

At last there was the entry, and the names they were looking for! Thomas Edward's parents were James Edward Ainsworth and Jane Ainsworth. Later, they traced a marriage certificate dated 1870. Jane's maiden name was Smith.

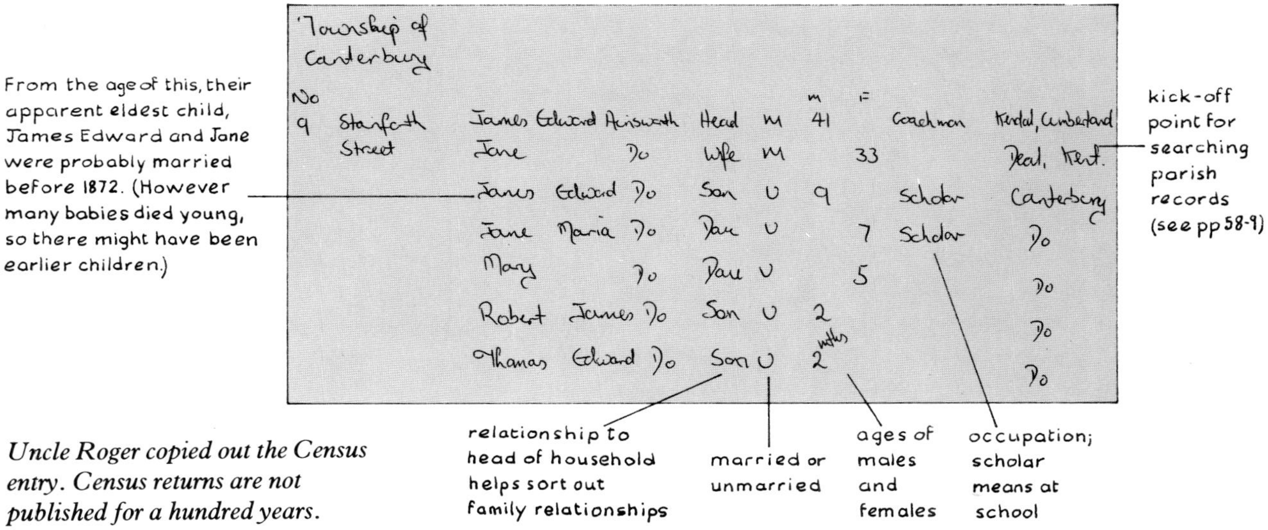

Uncle Roger copied out the Census entry. Census returns are not published for a hundred years.

The world of the 1840s

In this decade Sophie and Ben found that Britain continued to change from an agricultural to an industrial economy. Hundreds of people made or lost fortunes investing in new railway lines, spurred on by the examples of brilliant engineers like the Stephensons and Brunel.

At a cost of a penny a mile, all but the poorest could use the rail network, so increasingly they flocked in from the countryside to places like Manchester and Bradford to take up jobs in the growing industries.

The railways also helped the postal service to be speedier and more reliable than in previous decades when letters and parcels were delivered by the horse-drawn mail coaches. The first postage stamp ever, the Penny Black, was issued in 1840.

Communications generally had also been improved by the invention of the telegraph. Faster transatlantic crossings were made by the Cunard Steamship Company.

Stage coaches were still running in the 40s and penetrated many remoter quarters of the country unserved by railway lines. Hotels and inns were usually their pick-up points, where the horses were changed, and passengers could climb down from the lurching vehicle for a meal and a rest.

The best way to move most heavy goods was by water. Canals, first dug in the 1760s, had by the 1840s reached all over the country. Almost all the coal used in industry was carried on horse-drawn, wide barges like this one, or on narrowboats.

With so many coal fires, sweeping the chimney free of soot was essential. Little boys, sometimes as young as four or five, had to crawl up dark, narrow flues and sweep away the soot. Sometimes they suffocated or were even burned to death.

Events of the 1840s

Potato famine in Ireland made many poor people migrate to countries like America and Canada.

Convicted criminals were transported to Australia (often for trivial offences).

Gas lighting became common in town houses.

The first Christmas cards were sent, and Christmas trees were made popular in Britain by Prince Albert.

Discovery of gold in California led to the first of the great gold rushes.

The first anaesthetics were used for operations. Before then, yelling patients had their arms or legs sawn off while fully conscious.

Spinning machinery had been invented 100 years before, but the simple spinning wheel was still a familiar object in many poorer homes. Women spun cotton or wool fibres into yarn, which was then woven into cloth.

Parish registers

Sophie and Ben had already gleaned some information about one pair of Dad's paternal great-grandparents. According to the 1879 birth certificate of their daughter Caroline Louisa Muir, they were John Muir, a tailor, and Charlotte Muir, née Pugh. But Uncle Roger could not trace their marriage certificate at the General Register Office, even though he searched back for ten years from Caroline's birth. Nor, without an address, could he find the couple easily in the huge Bristol Census of 1881.

'I'll try the International Genealogical Index,' he said. 'The Mormon sect in America have, for their own religious reasons, photocopied many millions of names from British registers. Anybody can search their Indexes free.'

In the Mormons' London Regional Genealogical Library, Sophie and Ben helped him search the Indexes. These were kept on single pieces of film called microfiches, which had to be viewed through a special reading machine.

And there was the marriage – in Bristol in 1859, *twenty* years earlier. No wonder Uncle Roger couldn't find it! Probably John and Charlotte Muir had lots of children (as was common at the time) and Caroline Louisa was one of the later-born ones. Now, with an exact date, Uncle Roger could order the marriage certificate. Later he found John's birth there in 1837.

However, Charlotte Pugh was born *before* the central registration of births, deaths, and marriages. So they again tried the International Genealogical Index for Bristol, and found Charlotte in the parish of St Michael and All Angels.

•

Then Sophie and Ben turned to Dad's other pair of paternal great-grandparents. They knew that Dad's great-grandfather's name was William Trevor. They had learned this from the marriage certificate of his son William Trevor in 1899. (In order not to confuse the two Williams, they

This photo, sent by Grandad Trevor, had the faint pencilled word 'Julia' on the back. Sophie and Ben wondered if it was their great-great-grandmother, Julia Dawson.

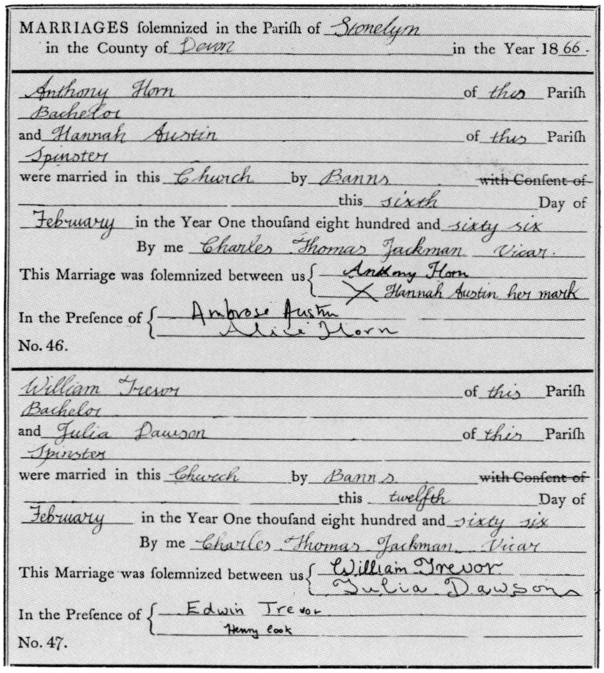

MARRIAGES ſolemnized in the Pariſh of Stonelym in the County of Devon in the Year 1866.

Anthony Horn of this Pariſh
Bachelor
and Hannah Austin of this Pariſh
Spinster
were married in this Church by Banns ~~with Conſent of~~
this sixth Day of
February in the Year One thouſand eight hundred and sixty six
By me Charles Thomas Jackman Vicar.
This Marriage was ſolemnized between us { Anthony Horn / X Hannah Austin her mark
In the Preſence of { Ambrose Austin / Alice Horn
No. 46.

William Trevor of this Pariſh
Bachelor
and Julia Dawson of this Pariſh
Spinster
were married in this Church by Banns ~~with Conſent of~~
this twelfth Day of
February in the Year One thouſand eight hundred and sixty six
By me Charles Thomas Jackman Vicar
This Marriage was ſolemnized between us { William Trevor / Julia Dawson
In the Preſence of { Edwin Trevor / Henry Cook
No. 47.

Parish record entry of the marriage of William Trevor 2 and Julia Dawson.

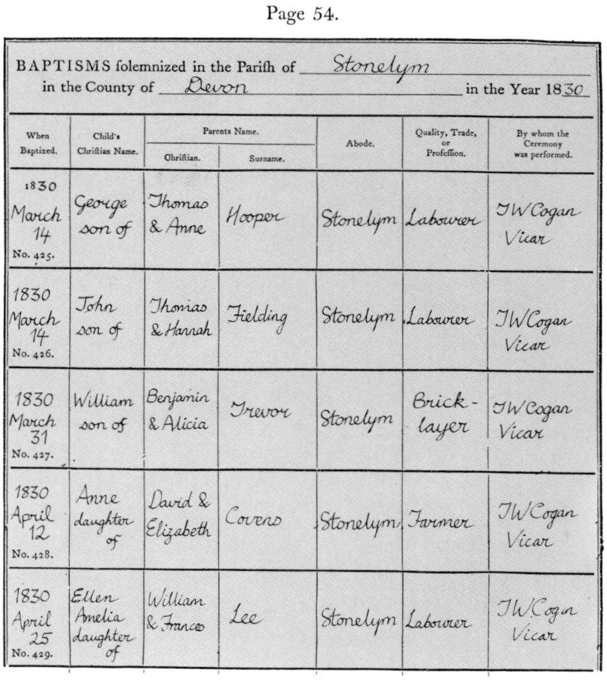

Page 54.

BAPTISMS ſolemnized in the Pariſh of Stonelym in the County of Devon in the Year 1830

When Baptized.	Child's Chriſtian Name.	Parents Name. Chriſtian.	Parents Name. Surname.	Abode.	Quality, Trade, or Profeſſion.	By whom the Ceremony was performed.
1830 March 14 No. 425.	George son of	Thomas & Anne	Hooper	Stonelym	Labourer	JW Cogan Vicar
1830 March 14 No. 426.	John son of	Thomas & Hannah	Fielding	Stonelym	Labourer	JW Cogan Vicar
1830 March 31 No. 427.	William son of	Benjamin & Alicia	Trevor	Stonelym	Bricklayer	JW Cogan Vicar
1830 April 12 No. 428.	Anne daughter of	David & Elizabeth	Covens	Stonelym	Farmer	JW Cogan Vicar
1830 April 25 No. 429.	Ellen Amelia daughter of	William & Frances	Lee	Stonelym	Labourer	JW Cogan Vicar

Parish record entry of the baptism of William Trevor 2, son of Benjamin Trevor.

called the son William 1, and the father William 2. Numbering this way round, they could add Williams 3, 4, 5 and so on, if they found other ones further back into the past.)

Luckily, at the time of the 1871 Census, the Trevors were still living at the address where William 1 was born. The Census showed William I was the eldest living child of William Trevor (William 2) aged 41, a mason, born in Stonelym, Devon, and of Julia Trevor, aged 35, a lace-maker, also from Stonelym.

Uncle Roger thought it would be fun to look them up in the actual parish records, if Sophie and Ben could persuade their parents to let them spend a week of the school holidays in Devon.

It was very exciting at the Devon County Record Office in Exeter when the actual old record books for the parish of St. Margaret's, Stonelym, were brought out. As with all original records, Uncle Roger handled them very carefully.

The handwriting was sometimes difficult to read, but at last they found what they were looking for. First the marriage of William Trevor 2 to Julia Dawson in 1866 at Stonelym, and then William and Julia's baptism entries – in 1830 and 1836 respectively. And, to their delight, William 2's father turned out to be a Benjamin Trevor!

'So you see, Ben, you *are* called after someone, after all,' said Uncle Roger. 'And now, if you like, you may carry on searching even further back. You'll probably find many more ancestors near Stonelym. Before the railways came, people didn't move about very much. Sometimes the trail will peter out. At other times your family history detective story could just go on and on, and get more and more fascinating.'

Sophie and Ben's family tree

William Trevor (2)
(s of Benjamin Trevor, bricklayer, and Alicia)
bapt 18/2/1830 in Stonelym, Devon
Mason

= Julia Dawson
(dau of Jonathan and Margaret Dawson)
bapt 7/1/1336 in Stonelym
Lacemaker
m 12/2/1865 in Stonelym

John Muir
(s of Edward Muir)
b 26/12/1837 in Bristol
Tailor

= Charlotte Pugh
(dau of Frederick Pugh, weaver)
b 2/1/1836 in Bristol
m 19/4/1859 in Bristol

James Edward Ainsworth
b 1840 in Kendal, Cumberland
Coachman

= Jane Smith
(dau of Robert Smith, shopkeeper)
b 1848 in Deal, Kent
m 25/12/1870

Henry Hardstone
(s of Ambrose Hardstone, Printer, and Harriet)
b 13/6/1840 in Maidstone
d 31/12/1892

= Mary Ann Body
(dau of Ross Body, newspaper proprietor, and Emily)
b 4/3/1849 in Maidstone
m 20/8/1875

William Trevor (1)
b 10/5/1870 in Bristol
Army, Boer War
Carpenter
d 28/8/1949 in Worcester

= Caroline Louisa Muir
b 2/11/1879 in Bristol
General maid
m 20/5/1899 in Bristol

Thomas Edward Ainsworth
b 3/2/1881 in Canterbury
Solicitor's clerk

= Emily Sophia Hardstone
b 28/1/1885 in Canterbury
Suffragette
m 20/3/1905 in Canterbury

Richard George Trevor
(Grandad Trevor)
b 16/2/1911 in Berkshire
Shop assistant
Soldier (Second World War)
Emigrated to New Zealand
Remarried (Mary Tomkins)
Bank manager (retired)

= Elsie Margot Ainsworth
(Granny Trevor)
b 4/8/1910 in Blackheath, London
Typist
m 9/6/1934
d 20/7/1944

Key to layout of family trees

A man and a woman linked by the sign = are married.

A vertical line from the sign = leads to a child of the marriage. (Sometimes, to help the appearance of that tree, the line turns horizontal before turning vertical again.)

Dates are given in the order day/month/year; e.g. 2/6/1977 means 2nd June 1977.

b born
bapt baptised
c circa (which means 'about this time')
d died
dau daughter
div divorced
m married
s son
? the following information is uncertain

Index

Henry William Grant
(s of William Grant, shopkeeper)
b 27/2/1859
Shopkeeper

= Victoria Fairburn Clark
(dau of George Clark, shop assistant)
b 14/6/1858
m 18/8/1879

Charles Langley
(s of Jeremiah Langley, builder)
b 11/2/1856 in Wendover, Herts.

= Sarah Elizabeth Welford
(dau of Clarence Welford, builder)
b 1859
m 23/4/1885 in Hemel Hempstead

Joseph Albert Stokes
(s of Albert Stokes, Mill owner)
b 1861 in Selby
Mill owner, Stokes Mill, Selby, Yorks.

= Emma Anne Burrows
(dau of Rev. Ernest Burrows, Clergyman)
b 1869 in Leeds
Teacher
m 10/9/1895 in Leeds

"Squire" Robert Markham of Ricking House
b ?1865 in ?Ricking, Lincs.
d 27/3/1932

= Lucy Mary Hammond
(dau of Frederick Hammond of Grantham)
b ?1867
m ?before 1892
d 12/8/1957

Reginald Sydney Grant
b 27/6/1895 in Birmingham
Soldier, First World War
Shoe factory worker
d 4/11/1963

= Florence Winifred Langley
b 12/8/1895 in Tring, Hertfordshire
Nurse, First World War
m 23/5/1920
d 27/7/1985

Wilfred Burrows Stokes
b 3/1/1901 in Selby, Yorkshire
Car salesman
RAF (Second World War)
d 10/5/1942

= Katherine Vera Markham ("Kate")
b 4/3/1900 in Ricking, Lincolnshire
'Flapper'
m 14/2/1923

William Eric Grant (Grandpa G)
b 15/9/1920 in Aylesbury, Buckinghamshire
Junior clerk, Ministry of Agriculture
Lieutenant, Army (Second World War)
Senior Civil Servant (retired)

= Katherine Eileen Stokes (Grandma G)
b 10/7/1924 in Ripon, Yorkshire
Doctor's receptionist
Wren (Second World War)
m 5/4/1946

Andrew Richard Trevor (Dad)
b 3/2/1940 in Dulwich, London
Engineer

= Elizabeth Katherine Grant (Mum)
b 24/1/1950 in York
Secretary
m 4/6/1968 in Harrogate

Mark Trevor
b 21/12/1969 in Africa

Sophie Trevor
b 29/9/1975 in Epsom, Surrey

Benjamin Trevor
b 2/6/1977 in Tonbridge, Kent